VEGAN
DESSERTS
WORLD.COM

Copyright © Lara Albrecht | www.vegandessertsworld.com

First Edition December, 2018

ISBN: 9781790749980

Imprint: Independently published

Favorite Desserts made VEGAN!

100 Sweet Seductive Recipes

Vegan baking, cooking, experimenting, and eating? It's a treat!

These pages are proof. Each recipe is specially created to provide exceptional taste and flavor. From cakes to cookies to baked and raw, this book proves that it feels good to be vegan. And it tastes delicious too!

Embrace exceptional flavors and fragrances.

Enjoy raw or baked.

Take a bite out of these specially designed vegan recipes.

From adaptations of traditional food to new innovations, we offer something for all palates.

Our sweet recipes evoke memories of favorite foods, favorite people, and favorite moments.

The 3 authors? Lara Albrecht, vegan chef and author, Catherine H. Barrington, the woman behind *Vegan Desserts World*, and Kathy Chrzaszcz, a registered holistic nutritionist and chef, put vigor and love, knowledge and responsibility, and flavor flavor flavor into cooking.

Going vegan has never tasted so good.

Introduction

Start your ovens and lick your lips: seriously delicious vegan desserts are in your future!

With these recipes, you can experience the benefits of eating cleaner, plant-based foods while still indulging and satisfying your sweet tooth. Despite popular belief, veganism isn't about limiting your diet; it's about indulging in compassionate eating. As long as you have the tools, tips, and tricks, there is no deprivation involved in this diet.

This book is filled with lots of variety and includes raw recipes, gluten-free, low-fat, easy to make selections, and our secret favorites, the ***Darling Recipes***. All of them are divided into colors.

 Darling Recipe Raw Gluten-Free Low Fat Easy

We had so much fun creating these recipes and we encourage you to have fun too: play around with different flours or sweeteners and experiment by switching up the ingredients. Don't just make a dish you'll like – create something you'll love!

With this book, you'll enjoy dessert without the hurt: pancakes, cupcakes, cinnamon rolls, crepes, and more – come see what we have in store!

Choose. Create. Devour. Repeat.

Now onto the moment you've been "baking" for.

We hope you're hungry.

Lara, Cathrine & Kathy

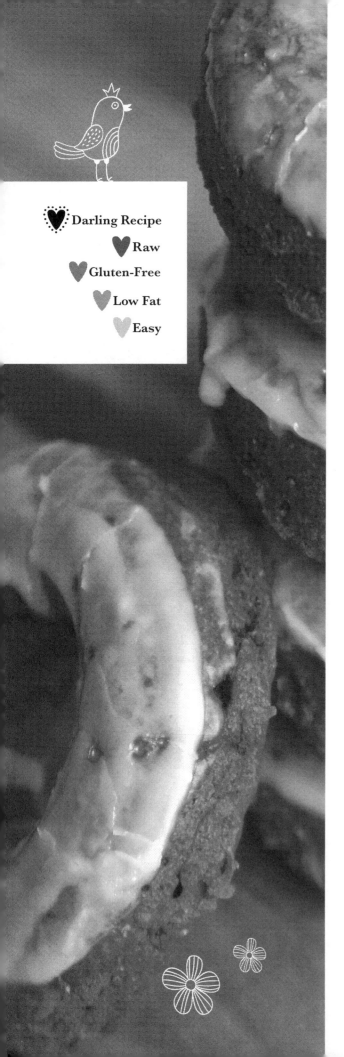

♥ Darling Recipe
♥ Raw
♥ Gluten-Free
♥ Low Fat
♥ Easy

Content

Mmm. Our Favorites, the Darlings of the Darlings!

Our 9 Favorite Ingredients ♥

...For Vegan Baking: Successful vegan baking requires knowledge of the basic staples that are at the heart of all this deliciousness. Perfecting a few tricks with these ingredients will help you become a master vegan baker!

Our Top 9 Staples:

1. Maple Syrup
2. Cane Sugar
3. Aquafaba
4. Full Fat Coconut Milk
5. Other Non-Dairy Milks
6. Flax Seeds
7. Dates
8. Coconut Oil
9. Cocoa Powder

Sweeteners: ♥

Maple Syrup

Maple syrup is our all-time favorite sweetener because of its taste and health benefits. It is our go-to when a recipe requires a liquid sweetener.

Cane Sugar

Cane sugar is the all-natural version of white sugar. Use cane sugar in equal parts to replace white sugar in any recipe.

Dates

Dates are a wonderful wholefood sweetener, go steady with them!

They are excellent to use when making raw treats (such as power balls and cheesecake). They also work great as caramel in desserts.

Egg Replacers:

There are several ways to substitute eggs in vegan baking. Our top 2 favorites are aquafaba and ground flax.

Aquafaba

Aquafaba is a magical ingredient. It perfectly mimics egg whites in most baking recipes. Aquafaba is very similar in texture to egg whites, but it can be used in vegan baking to replace whole eggs as well. It helps create the moisture in baking. It can even be whipped to make meringue, producing an identical feel to eggs.

Flax Seeds

It's hard to believe a tiny seed can be packed with so much health! These mighty morsels are wonderful to use as egg replacers.

Soak ground flax in a little bit of water and it will gelatinize into an egg-like texture. To do this, add 1 tbsp of ground flax to a small bowl, along with 3 tbsp of water. Whisk it to combine and allow it to sit for ten minutes. This measurement is the equivalent of one egg.

♥ Milk Replacements:

Full Fat Coconut Milk

This type of milk is often found in a can, labelled as full fat or rich coconut milk. It has a higher fat content than most other coconut milks, which makes it ideal for recipes that need to be richer. You can use it in baking or to make vegan ice cream.

Other Non-Dairy Milks

There are many non-dairy milks that can replace regular milk in baking. These options include almond, oat, hemp, coconut, hazelnut, soy, flax, rice, and several other alternatives. 99% of the time they are completely interchangeable. For best results, stick to unflavored and unsweetened milk, so the taste of the recipe isn't altered. Almond milk and soy milk work well in most recipes.

Other: ♥

Cocoa Powder

Many people think that chocolate isn't vegan, and therefore cocoa isn't vegan. But plain cocoa or cacao powder is completely vegan – taste buds, rejoice! Just look for brands that only contain cocoa powder and no other ingredients (not all brands are vegan). We love the *Camino* brand of cocoa powder because it's not only healthy but also Fairtrade certified.

Coconut Oil

Coconut oil is a wonderful oil for baking. You can use it to replace butter and regular vegetable oils in baking recipes. It has a melting point of 24 degrees C. Because it's multi-talented (it can be liquid or solid), it is particularly helpful in a variety of recipes. It's the star of the show in truffles or fudge – when chilled, the coconut oil solidifies, producing a wonderful base.

Other ingredients are important too, even if they haven't quite reached "staple status." These include: All-purpose flour, baking powder, baking soda, vegan butter, vanilla extract, vegan chocolate chips, apple sauce, and apple cider vinegar. Apple cider vinegar is excellent for recipes like waffles, pancakes, and the like, because it turns regular milk into buttermilk.

Tips for Low-Fat or Fat-Free Vegan Baking

If you like to use minimal fat when cooking, there are a few ingredients that help maintain moisture and enhance flavor. **Aquafaba** is one of these ingredients (see, it's magical!). Use this as your preferred egg replacer in vegan baking (it has virtually no fat). When you need to replace oil in cakes, muffins, and loaves, try unsweetened **apple sauce** (substitute it equally). Apple sauce gives you the moisture you need without the "heavy."

Free the Gluten!

Many recipes in this book are gluten-free, while others can be made gluten-free by replacing the flour with a gluten-free flour substitute. It should be noted that the baking time may differ if gluten-free substitutes are used. Oats are not always gluten-free. That's why the recipes in this book that contain oats are not labeled as such. If required, make sure the oat products you use are gluten-free.

Sugar? Vegan Sweet Icing on the Cake

You love your sweets – we don't blame you! The availability of sweeteners is amazing. The alternatives range from unbleached whole cane sugar to maple syrup, from coconut blossom sugar to syrup and dates. Every well-stocked supermarket or drugstore offers these items.

A note on snow-white table sugar:
The bleaching process and the use of any excipients, decide whether it is a true vegan food. If you want to be sure, send a product inquiry to the manufacturer or use unrefined cane sugar instead.

What Other Supplies are Required?

Appliances, Machines, and Tools

Not everyone has a kitchen full of equipment straight out of SkyMall, but **you don't need** high-tech for high-flavor vegan cooking.
These 100 recipes only require the basics. We love to use a stand mixer to mix different batters and icings. A high-powered blender such as a Vitamix or Blendtec will work wonders. It makes sauces, icings, and other foods perfectly smooth. It saves you time, too.

Occasionally, a food processor is helpful when a blender won't cut it. Recipes for power balls or raw cake crusts work better with this machine. A food processor is always helpful when pulsing together ingredients like nuts and dates.

11

Chapter 1

Desserts ... Raw Raw Raw!

Cheer on these recipes: "Raw! Raw! Raw! Give me a plate!" They're easy to make and attractive to those with dietary restrictions (most are gluten-free). Pack these in your lunch pail and pack your day with energy.

No-Bake Brownies

| 1 | **Nutrition Info Per Serving:** 30g Carbs, 5g Protein, 15g Fat, 270 Calories |

We know, we know - we had you at "no baking"! Ditch the oven for some lovin' of these delicious treats! They're filled with walnuts and dates, making a delectable dessert. Rich, quick, and raw, raw, raw!

No-Bake Brownies

Makes:
9 Medium Brownies

Prep Time:
15 Minutes
Cook Time:
0 Minutes

Ingredients

Brownie Layer
- 2 cups packed pitted dates, such as Medjool
- 1 ½ cups walnuts, unsalted
- ½ cup cocoa powder, unsweetened
- 1 tsp vanilla extract

Chocolate Ganache
- 2 tbsp coconut oil, melted
- ¼ cup cocoa powder, unsweetened
- ¼ cup pure maple syrup
- 1 tsp vanilla

Directions

1. In a food processor, blend the dates, walnuts, cocoa powder, and vanilla extract, until the mixture comes together evenly. The walnut pieces should be small and the batter should be slightly sticky.
2. Line an 8x8-inch square baking pan with parchment or wax paper. Press the brownie batter into the pan and spread out evenly. Set aside.
3. Melt the coconut oil in a microwave or saucepot until just melted.
4. In a bowl, combine all of the ganache ingredients and whisk until smooth.

5. Pour the ganache on top of the brownie batter and tip the pan from side to side to spread the ganache evenly.
6. Refrigerate for at least 1 hour before serving.

15

Raw Mocha Cheesecake

2	**Nutrition Info Per Serving:** 25g Carbs, 7g Protein, 19g Fat, 302 Calories

A creamy dream of coffee and cocoa. If you're looking for a chocolatey espresso-flavored dessert, then you've struck gold with another Darling Recipe! This mocha cheesecake is a real treat for coffee lovers – it captivates, not only with its appearance, but with its irresistible creaminess. Well, who wants a piece?

Makes:
10 Servings

Prep Time:
25 Minutes
Freeze Time:
5 Hours

Ingredients

Crust
- 1 ¼ cups soft dates such as Medjool or Deglet Noor
- 1 cup hazelnuts
- ⅓ cup shredded coconut, unsweetened
- 2 tbsp cocoa powder, unsweetened
- 1 tsp ground coffee
- 1 tsp vanilla extract
- Pinch of salt

Filling
- 1 ½ cups cashews
- ¾ cup strong brewed coffee
- ½ cup full fat coconut milk from a can
- ¼ cup + 1 tbsp maple syrup
- 1 tbsp + 2 tsp cocoa powder, unsweetened
- 1 ½ tsp vanilla extract
- Pinch of salt
- Coffee beans and coffee grounds for garnish

Directions

1. Add all of the crust ingredients into a food processor and blend for 23 minutes until the mixture is well combined and starts to ball up. The mixture should be slightly crumbly but stick together when pinched.
2. Press the crust ingredients into the bottom and sides of a 9inch pie pan or torte pan. Spread the mixture evenly and form a nice crust up the sides of the pan.
3. Blend all of the filling ingredients in a high-powered blender until smooth.
   If you don't have a powerful blender, you will want to soak the cashews for a few hours to soften them.
4. Pour the filling ingredients into the pie pan and spread it out evenly. Garnish with a light sprinkle of coffee grounds and decorate with coffee beans if desired. Freeze for at least 5 hours before slicing. Store in the freezer until ready to serve. Thaw for at least 10 minutes before serving.

Chocolate Dessert

Chia Pudding

3 | **Nutrition Info Per Serving:** 40g Carbs, 15g Protein, 34g Fat, 520 Calories

Chia pudding is just as tasty as traditional pudding, but it offers the added perk of health benefits. It's filled with fiber, making it a great snack at any time of day. This recipe, paired with a layer of velvety chocolate, will leave you going back for seconds (thirds too).

Chocolate Dessert Chia Pudding

Makes:
2 Servings

Prep Time:
35 Minutes
Cook Time:
0 Minutes

Ingredients

- 2 tbsp chia seeds
- 1 cup non-dairy milk, unsweetened (e.g. almond milk)
- 1 cup cashews
- ¾ cup water
- 3 tbsp maple syrup
- 2 tbsp cocoa powder, unsweetened
- 1 tsp vanilla extract

Directions

1. Soak the chia seeds in the non-dairy milk. Whisk it together for a few minutes until the chia seeds soak up most of the milk. Set aside in the fridge for a minimum of 30 minutes and stir occasionally.

2. If you don't have a high-powered blender, you will want to soak your cashews for at least 3 hours in hot water before blending the pudding. Drain the water and blend all of the remaining ingredients in a blender until smooth. If you have a high-powered blender, you can skip the soaking.

3. When the chia seeds have soaked up the milk and the mixture is nice and thick, layer the chia seeds and chocolate pudding in a bowl or cup. Feel free to add toppings such as fresh fruit, nuts, or seeds, etc.

No-Bake *Nanaimo Bars*

| 4 | **Nutrition Info Per Serving:** 51g Carbs, 11g Protein, 40g Fat, 595 Calories |

Oh Canada! Nanaimo is a classic treat that hails from British Columbia. This recipe is the raw, unbaked version that's packed with health (walnuts, coconut, and cashews). It's easy to make, but requires a bit of freezing. Not surprising for a Canadian dish.

Ingredients

Base Layer

- 2 cups soft pitted dates, such as Medjool
- 2 cups walnuts, unsalted
- 1 cup coconut shreds, unsweetened
- 2 tbsp cocoa powder, unsweetened
- ½ tsp vanilla extract
- Pinch of salt

Custard Layer

- 2 cups cashews, unsalted and unroasted
- ½ cup warm water
- ¼ cup maple syrup
- 2 tsp vanilla extract

Chocolate Layer

- ¼ cup coconut oil
- ½ cup cocoa powder, unsweetened
- ½ cup maple syrup
- 1 tsp vanilla extract

Directions

1. Line an 8x8-inch baking sheet with parchment paper. Ensure there is enough paper hanging over the sides so that you can lift the entire contents out later.
2. Add all of the base layer ingredients into a food processor. Process until the mixture combines nicely together.
3. Press the mixture into the bottom of the baking pan so it is spread evenly. Set aside.
4. In a high-powered blender, blend all of the custard ingredients until very smooth. If the mixture isn't blending enough, add additional warm water, a few teaspoons at a time, until the blender runs smoothly.
5. Pour the custard layer on top of the base layer and spread out evenly. Place in the freezer for 1 hour.

No-Bake Nanaimo Bars

Makes:
9 Bars

Prep Time:
25 Minutes

Freeze Time:
1 Hour +30 Minutes

6. When 1 hour has passed, melt the coconut oil in a small pot until just melted. Take the pot off the heat and add the rest of the chocolate layer ingredients. Whisk until smooth.
7. Take the baking sheet out of the freezer and pour the chocolate on top. Tip the pan from side to side so the chocolate can spread evenly.
8. Place the pan in the freezer for about 30 minutes, or until the chocolate is set. Cut into squares and serve. Store leftovers in the freezer.

Lemon Zest Chia Pudding

| 5 | **Nutrition Info Per Serving:** 24g Carbs, 4g Protein, 9g Fat, 211 Calories |

Probably the healthiest pudding in the world, a modern trendy breakfast, and a healthy superfood spoon snack: Chia pudding. Our creamy-fresh version with cashews and lemon will sweeten your morning right after getting up. Stirred together at lightning speed, quilting overnight, the pudding stays fresh in the fridge for up to a week.

Low-Fat, Raw, Gluten-Free, Easy

Lemon Zest Chia Pudding

Makes:
2 Servings

Prep Time:
35 Minutes
Cook Time:
0 Minutes

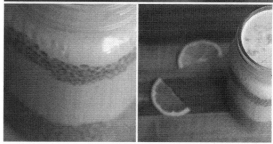

Ingredients

Chia Layer
- 1 cup non-dairy milk, unsweetened (e.g. almond milk)
- ¼ cup chia seeds

Lemon Pudding Layer
- 1 cup cashews
- ½ cup non-dairy milk, unsweetened
- ¼ cup lemon juice
- 3 tbsp maple syrup
- 2 tsp lemon zest
- ¼ tsp vanilla extract

Directions

1. Soak the chia seeds in the almond milk. Whisk vigorously for about 5 minutes, then set aside in the fridge to soak for at least 30 minutes or longer. Stir every few minutes. You can even leave this in the fridge overnight and prepare the rest of the ingredients the next day if desired.
2. Blend all of the lemon pudding layer ingredients in a high-powered blender until smooth.
3. Layer the soaked chia and the pudding in a cup or bowl. Top with additional lemon zest or other toppings if desired.

The Best Chocolate Pudding Torte

| 6 | **Nutrition Info Per Serving:** 36g Carbs, 5g Protein, 16g Fat, 306 Calories |

Can the words chocolate, pie, pudding, and healthy be mentioned in one sentence? Dear sweet lovers, this decadent cake is one of our absolute favorites. It is raw, free of extra baking oil and refined sugar, is gluten-free, and packs a ton of rich chocolatey flavor. Perfect if you're in the mood for chocolate.

The Best Chocolate Pudding Torte

Makes:
8 Servings

Prep Time:
15 Minutes
Cook Time:
0 Minutes

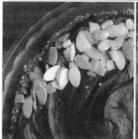

Ingredients

Crust
- 1 cup soft dates such as Medjool or Deglet Noor
- ⅓ cup hazelnuts
- ⅓ cup almonds
- ⅓ cup shredded coconut, unsweetened
- ½ tsp vanilla extract
- Pinch of salt

Pudding
- 2 large avocados (or 3 small)
- ¾ cup maple syrup
- ½ cup + 2 tbsp cocoa powder, unsweetened
- 1 ½ tsp vanilla extract
- Pinch of salt
- Almond slivers for garnish

Directions

1. In a food processor, blend all of the crust ingredients for about 3 minutes, until it starts to stick together and ball up.
2. Pour the crust into an 8-inch pie pan or torte pan. Press the crust to form an even layer on the bottom and about an inch up the sides.
3. Blend all of the pudding ingredients, except for the almond slivers, in a blender until smooth. If you use ripe avocados you shouldn't taste the avocado. But if you do taste an undertone of avocado, you can add more cocoa, maple syrup, or vanilla to taste.
4. Pour the pudding into the crust and spread it out evenly. Garnish with the almond slivers (you could also garnish with coconut shreds).
5. Chill the torte in the fridge for at least 30 minutes before slicing. Store in the fridge.

Pumpkin Cheesecake

| 7 | **Nutrition Info Per Serving:** 20g Carbs, 10g Protein, 22g Fat, 318 Calories |

Creamy, sweet, perfectly spiced, the Pumpkin Cheesecake is the perfect dessert for the fall. The pumpkin gives the cake the creaminess, the beautiful orange-yellowish color, and the delicious taste. The cake is awesome to make ahead of time, because you can store it and serve it straight out of the freezer.

Dessert Idea for Thanksgiving

Ingredients

- 1 ½ cups almonds, ground
- 1 cup packed soft dates
- 1 tbsp cocoa powder, unsweetened
- 1 tsp vanilla extract
- 3 cups cashews
- 1 cup canned pumpkin purée*
- ⅔ cup maple syrup
- 2 tsp pumpkin spice
- 1 tsp vanilla extract

Directions

1. Line an 8x8-inch square pan with parchment paper and set aside.
2. In a food processor, blend the almonds until you form a flour.
3. Add the dates, cocoa powder, vanilla and blend until the mixture comes together.
4. Take the dough and press it into the bottom of the pan, spreading evenly.
5. In a high-powered blender, blend the cashews, pumpkin purée, maple syrup, pumpkin spice, and vanilla until very smooth.
6. Pour this mixture into the pan and spread evenly.
7. Freeze for at least 2 hours and serve (it's best to cut it into even pieces before freezing). Store in the freezer.

* It is easy to make pumpkin purée from scratch yourself. You have two options:

In the oven: Wash a Hokkaido pumpkin and cut in half (do not peel!). Remove the insides. Place the pumpkin halves with the cut side down on a baking sheet lined with baking paper. Bake at 350°F until a fork can easily pierce the pumpkin (about 1 to 1 ½ h). Remove from the oven, allow to cool, and puree with a little water.

Raw, Gluten-Free

Pumpkin Cheesecake

Makes:
12 Mini Cheesecakes

Prep Time:
15 Minutes
Freeze Time:
2 Hours

In water: Wash a Hokkaido pumpkin and cut into pieces (do not peel!). Remove the insides. Cook in boiling water until the pumpkin is soft (about 20 minutes). Then dump the water and purée everything until it is the consistency of apple sauce.

Chocolate

Avocado Mousse

| 8 | **Nutrition Info Per Serving:** 36g Carbs, 8g Protein, 25g Fat, 410 Calories |

Avocados are a superfood – a fruit that practically wears a cape. But it's not just about health: adding avocado to a dish, ups the flavor and the consistency. This mousse proves that! This is a treat you'll want to meet: it's packed with antioxidants, "good" fats, and loads of protein.

Chocolate Avocado Mousse

Makes:
2 Servings

Prep Time:
5 Minutes

Cook Time:
0 Minutes

Ingredients

- 2 medium ripe avocados
- ½ cup cocoa powder
- ½ cup non-dairy milk, unsweetened (e.g. almond milk)
- ¼ cup maple syrup
- 1 tsp vanilla extract
- ½ cup fresh raspberries

Directions

1. In a blender, blend all of the ingredients, except for the raspberries, until smooth.
2. Pour into a glass and serve right away, or chill first. Serve with fresh raspberries.

No-Bake Donut Holes

| 9 | **Nutrition Info Per Serving:** 15g Carbs, 2g Protein, 3g Fat, 93 Calories |

The Donut Holes are one of our Darling Recipes in this book. They are made with mostly raw ingredients and contain a lot of cashews, dates and oats – a treat! The proof is in front of you.

Dessert Idea for Donut Day (every first Friday of June)

Makes:
14 Donut Holes

Prep Time:
45 Minutes
Cook Time:
0 Minutes

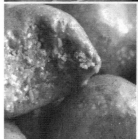

Ingredients

Batter
- ⅔ cup rolled oats
- ⅔ cup cashews
- ½ cup dates
- ¼ cup maple syrup
- 2 tsp cinnamon
- 1 tsp vanilla

Glaze
- 6 tbsp powdered cane sugar
- 3 tsp water
- 1 tsp cinnamon

Directions

1. In a food processor, blend all of the ingredients until very well combined. Pulse if needed.
2. Line a small pan with parchment. Roll the dough into about 14 small balls. Place them on the parchment lined pan and freeze for 10-15 minutes.
3. While the donut holes are in the freezer, make your glaze by whisking together all of the glaze ingredients in a small bowl until smooth and combined.
4. Take the donut holes out of the freezer and dip each ball into the glaze to coat with an even, thin layer. Place them back on the parchment and allow to freeze for another 20 minutes, or until the glaze is set.
5. Enjoy and store in the fridge if you haven't eaten them all!

Zesty Lemon
Energy Bites

10	**Nutrition Info Per Serving:** 7g Carbs, 5g Protein, 12g Fat, 158 Calories

These energy balls are ideal for any vegan on the go. They're filled with nutrients that keep you thriving throughout the day. The next time someone asks you where you get your protein, put one of these treats in their mouth (or offer them one politely – that works too).

Zesty Lemon Energy Bites

Makes:
9 Energy Balls

Prep Time:
10 Minutes

Cook Time:
0 Minutes

Ingredients

- 2 cups slivered almonds
- Zest of 1 lemon
- 2-3 tbsp maple syrup
- 1 tbsp lemon juice
- 1 tsp vanilla

Directions

1. Blend the almonds in a food processor until they turn into flour.
2. Add the rest of the ingredients and blend until combined.
3. Form the mixture into small balls with your hands. Enjoy!

Chapter 2

Cakes, Cupcakes, and Donuts

From a child's birthday party to a potluck, these recipes make excellent dishes to share with friends. You can also make them for no reason at all – they're savory "just because you're conscious" creations.

Coconut Carrot Cake

11	**Nutrition Info Per Serving:** 65g Carbs, 6g Protein, 27g Fat, 534 Calories

If you're not a fan of carrot cake, then sticking to regular carrots may be a better option. But, if you enjoy the dessert, then this is the recipe for you! It's very easy and quick to make, and is packed with good health: carrots, walnuts, and coconut. Will it improve your eyesight? Make it and "see"!

Ingredients

- 2 cups all-purpose flour
- 2 tsp baking powder
- 2 tsp baking soda
- 1 tsp cinnamon
- 1 ¼ cups coconut sugar or brown sugar
- ¾ cup vegan butter, melted
- ½ cup orange juice, unsweetened
- 1 tsp vanilla extract
- 3 cups carrots, shredded
- ¾ cup walnuts, chopped into small pieces
- ½ cup shredded coconut, unsweetened

Glaze
- ⅓ cup powdered cane sugar
- 1 tsp water

Directions

1. Preheat the oven to 350 degrees F and grease a 9-inch round baking pan with vegan butter. Set aside.
2. In a large bowl, sift together the flour, baking powder, baking soda, and cinnamon. Whisk until combined and set aside.
3. In a medium bowl, whisk together the sugar, melted vegan butter, orange juice, and vanilla extract.
4. Add shredded carrots into the wet mixture and mix to combine.
5. Add the wet ingredients to the dry ingredients and mix together until combined.
6. Fold chopped walnuts and coconut into the mixture.
7. Pour the mixture into the pan and bake for 45 minutes, or until a toothpick inserted comes out clean. Cool the cake in the pan until it is cool enough to transfer to a wire rack, to cool completely.

Darling Recipe

Coconut Carrot Cake

Makes:
8 Servings

Prep Time:
20 Minutes
Cook Time:
45 Minutes

8. When the cake is cooled, make your glaze by whisking together the powdered sugar and water. Spread the glaze on top of the cake. Sprinkle additional coconut shreds on top of the cake before the glaze sets.

NumberOne
Chocolate Cupcakes

12	**Nutrition Info Per Serving:** 46g Carbs, 4g Protein, 17g Fat, 349 Calories

This recipe is our top favorite in the book! Not only do these cupcakes summon the flavor of birthdays of yore, but they're extremely easy to make.
Call on this recipe when you need a last-minute treat. It'll be ready in three, two, one... yummy.

Ingredients

Batter

- 1 ¼ cups all-purpose flour
- ⅓ cup cocoa powder, unsweetened
- 1 tsp baking soda
- Pinch of salt
- 1 cup warm water
- 1 cup cane sugar
- ⅓ cup vegan butter, melted
- 1 tsp lemon juice
- 1 tsp vanilla extract

Icing

- 1 ½ cups cocoa powder, unsweetened
- ½ cup coconut oil, melted
- ¾ cup maple syrup
- 1 tsp vanilla extract

Directions

1. Preheat the oven to 350 degrees F. Line a cupcake pan with 12 cupcake liners and set aside.
2. In a medium bowl, sift together the flour, cocoa powder, baking soda, and salt. Whisk to combine and set aside.
3. In another medium bowl, combine the water, butter, sugar, lemon juice, and vanilla. Whisk together until smooth.
4. Add the wet to the dry ingredients and whisk until combined.
5. Distribute the batter evenly between the 12 cupcake liners. Bake for 18 minutes, or until a toothpick inserted comes out clean.
6. Allow the cupcakes to cool completely.

Makes:
12 Cupcakes

Prep Time:
20 Minutes
Cook Time:
18 Minutes

7. When the cupcakes are fully cooled, make your icing by whisking together all of the icing ingredients in a small bowl until smooth and combined. Spread on the muffins and enjoy!

Easter Sponge Cake

13	**Nutrition Info Per Serving:** 53g Carbs, 3g Protein, 9g Fat, 314 Calories

Fluffy, juicy – a dream... This sponge cake is just like the cake my grandma makes every Easter! Polish tradition is to make many different treats and place them in a decorative Easter basket to be blessed on Easter Saturday. The sponge cake with raisins is always a very special highlight.

Dessert Idea for Easter

Easter Sponge Cake

Makes:
8 Servings

Prep Time:
20 Minutes
Cook Time:
40 Minutes

Ingredients

- ½ cup raisins
- 1 ¾ cups all-purpose flour
- 1 tsp baking soda
- 1 tsp cinnamon
- Pinch of salt
- 1 cup cane sugar
- 1 cup water
- ⅓ cup coconut oil, melted
- 1 tbsp apple cider vinegar
- 1 tsp vanilla
- 1 tbsp powdered cane sugar

Directions

1. Preheat your oven to 350 degrees F. Grease a Bundt cake pan with a little bit of coconut oil and set aside.
2. Soak the raisins in hot water in a small bowl for 20 minutes.
3. While the raisins are soaking, whisk together the flour, baking soda, cinnamon, and salt in a medium bowl and set aside.
4. In another medium bowl, whisk together the cane sugar, water, coconut oil, vinegar, and vanilla.
5. Combine the wet and the dry ingredients and whisk until combined.
6. Drain the raisins from the water and fold them into the batter.

7. Pour the batter into the pan and bake for 40 minutes, or until a toothpick inserted comes out clean.
8. Cool completely and sift 1-2 tbsp powdered sugar on top before slicing.

Chocolate Log

| 14 | **Nutrition Info Per Serving:** 32g Carbs, 3g Protein, 16g Fat, 283 Calories |

The Chocolate Log is the perfect dessert to celebrate World Vegan Day. The International World Vegan Day takes place every year on the 1st of November to celebrate the plant-based lifestyle of the world. We congratulate all amazing vegans! What would be better suited than this cake in the form of a chocolatey tree trunk?

Dessert Idea for World Vegan Day (1st of November)

Ingredients

Batter

- ¾ cup aquafaba
- ½ cup cane sugar
- 2 tbsp apple sauce, unsweetened
- 1 tsp vanilla extract
- ½ cup all-purpose flour
- ¼ cup + 3 tbsp cocoa powder
- 1 tsp baking powder
- ¾ tsp baking soda
- Coconut oil for greasing the pan
- Powdered cane sugar for dusting

Frosting

- 1 ½ cups chocolate chips
- ⅓ cup + 2 tbsp powdered cane sugar
- ¼ cup + 2 tbsp non-dairy milk, unsweetened
- ¼ cup + 2 tbsp coconut oil
- 1 ½ tsp vanilla extract

Directions

1. Preheat the oven to 390 degrees F. Grease a swiss roll pan with coconut oil. Line the bottom of the pan and grease the top of the parchment as well so the cake doesn't stick.
2. In a stand mixer, beat the aquafaba on medium speed until it becomes foamy.
3. Add the sugar, apple sauce, and vanilla extract and beat to combine.
4. Add the flour, baking powder, cocoa powder, and baking soda, and mix until combined.
5. Pour the batter into the pan. Spread it out evenly. Tap the sides of the pan so that the batter is evenly distributed.
6. Bake for 10 minutes.
7. Line a cutting board with a clean tea towel.
8. Remove the cake from the oven. Lightly dust with powdered sugar. Cool for 5 minutes.
9. Gently flip the cake onto the cutting board lined with the tea towel. Dust this side of the

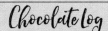

Chocolate Log

Makes:
12 Servings

Prep Time:
1 Hour
Cook Time:
10 Minutes

cake with powdered sugar. Use the tea towel to gently roll the cake with the towel inside, starting from one of the long sides.
10. While the cake is cooling, make your frosting. Add all of the frosting ingredients into a medium saucepan and melt on medium heat. Whisk until the ingredients are fully combined.
11. Pour the frosting into the bowl of your stand mixer. Place in freezer to firm up.
12. When the frosting is cool enough, place the bowl in the stand mixer. Beat it on medium/high for about 2 min.
13. Unroll the cake and frost the inside of the cake with a good layer of frosting. You want to use around ⅔ of the frosting for the inside.
14. Roll the cake and transfer it to a serving plate. Cut ⅓ of the cake on an angle and assemble this piece on the side of the cake to form a "branch".
15. Frost and run your knife in long streaks to create the look of tree bark. Dust with powdered sugar and serve.

Coffee Cake

| 15 | **Nutrition Info Per Serving:** 68g Carbs, 4g Protein, 22g Fat, 488 Calories |

Coffee? Awesome. Cake? Um, yeah! Put them together and it's hard to go wrong. Whether you make this treat for a group of friends or curl up with a good book and a slice, it makes delicious company. Eat comfortably with this comfort food.

Ingredients

- 2 ½ cups all-purpose flour
- 1 ½ tsp + ½ tsp cinnamon
- 1 tsp baking soda
- 1 tsp baking powder
- 1 cup coconut sugar
- ½ cup cane sugar
- ¾ cup coconut oil, solid
- 1 cup non-dairy milk, unsweetened (e.g. almond milk)
- ½ cup non-dairy yogurt, unsweetened
- ½ cup strong brewed coffee
- 2 tsp vanilla extract
- 1 tsp apple cider vinegar

Directions

1. Preheat the oven to 350 degrees F. Grease a Bundt cake pan with coconut oil and set aside.
2. In a medium bowl, sift together flour, 1 ½ tsp cinnamon, baking soda, baking powder, coconut sugar, and cane sugar.
3. Add the solid coconut oil into the flour mixture. Use a pastry cutter to combine the mixture, until it is crumbly and clumps still remain. You can use your hands, but you need to work fast so the coconut oil doesn't melt.
4. Take 1 cup of this mixture and put it in a separate bowl. Add the remaining ½ tsp of cinnamon, mix until combined, and set aside.
5. Mix together the flour mixture in the large bowl until little to no clumps of coconut oil remain.
6. In a small bowl, whisk together the milk, yogurt, coffee, vanilla, and apple cider vinegar.
7. Add the liquid to the flour mixture in the large bowl. Whisk until combined and no clumps remain.
8. Pour the cake batter into the Bundt cake pan. Pour the crumble mixture on top, press in.

Low-Fat

Coffee Cake

Makes:
8 Servings

Prep Time:
20 Minutes
Cook Time:
60-70 Minutes

9. Bake for 60-70 minutes, or until a toothpick inserted comes out clean.
10. Allow the cake to cool before transferring it out of the pan. When it is cool enough, transfer the cake onto a wire rack. Serve and enjoy!

Apple Walnut Loaf

16 | **Nutrition Info Per Serving:** 66g Carbs, 7g Protein, 5g Fat, 344 Calories

Pink clouds and butterflies in bread heaven. Do you love walnuts AND apples? Then our yummy bread recipe is just right for you. How delicious it smells! This apple and walnut bread powerhouse is naturally sweetened with dates, raisins, and 5 apples, and is therefore particularly juicy. A top candidate for fall and Christmas, that's for sure!

Apple Walnut Loaf

Makes:
10 Slices

Prep Time:
25 Minutes
Cook Time:
55 Minutes

Ingredients

- ½ cup soft dates, packed
- ½ cup hot water
- 5 large apples, peeled and cored
- 1 cup raisins
- ½ cup walnuts, chopped
- 4 cups all-purpose flour
- 1 ½ tsp baking soda
- 1 tbsp cocoa powder, unsweetened
- 1 tsp cinnamon

Directions

1. Preheat your oven to 350 degrees F. Grease a loaf pan with coconut oil and set aside.
2. Soak the dates in the hot water in a small bowl and set aside.
3. Peel and core 5 large apples. Grate the apples into a large bowl. Add the raisins and walnuts, stir to combine, and set aside.
4. In a medium bowl, whisk together the flour, baking soda, cocoa powder, and cinnamon. Set aside.
5. Blend the soaked dates with the water until smooth. Add the date paste into the dry ingredients and mix until just combined.
6. Add the apple mixture to the flour mix and combine with your hands to form a dough.

7. Press the dough evenly into the loaf pan and bake for 55 minutes, or until a toothpick inserted comes out clean (or if it sounds hollow when you knock on it).
8. Allow the loaf to cool completely before slicing. Enjoy!

Cheesecake

17	**Nutrition Info Per Serving:** 42g Carbs, 8g Protein, 15g Fat, 318 Calories

The New York style cheesecake is an iconic dessert, in fact possibly one of the most famous desserts in the world! With entire restaurants dedicated just to this one treat, you know it's a favorite among most. We topped ours with a blueberry sauce, but you could flavor yours any way you like.

Cheesecake

Makes:
12 Slices

Prep Time:
15 Minutes
Cook Time:
45 Minutes

Ingredients

Crust
- ½ cup brown sugar
- 1 cup rolled oats, dry
- 3 tbsp melted coconut oil
- ¼ tsp salt

Filling
- 2 cups cashews
- 400ml can full-fat coconut milk
- 1 14oz can chickpeas
- ⅔ cup maple syrup
- ¼ cup + 2 tbsp lemon juice
- 1 tbsp lemon zest
- 1 tsp vanilla extract

Directions

1. Preheat the oven to 350 degrees F. Grease a 9-inch springform pan and set aside.
2. Begin my making the crust. Blend the oats in a food processor until they resemble a flour. Add the sugar and salt and blend again to combine. Run the food processor and drizzle in the melted oil. Blend until the mixture comes together nicely. Press this crust evenly into the bottom of the pan.
3. Blend all of the filling ingredients in a high-powered blender until smooth. This may take a few minutes.

4. Pour the filling into the pan. Bake the cheesecake for 45 minutes. Cool completely before removing from the pan and serving. Feel free to top with things like fruit sauce, chocolate, fresh berries, and much more!

Sugar-Free WOW Apple Cake

| 18 | **Nutrition Info Per Serving:** 42g Carbs, 4g Protein, 30g Fat, 467 Calories |

The scent of cinnamon, roasted almonds, and warm apples makes this dessert a wonderful alternative to sugary recipes. No special occasion needed though! It's still sweet, but comes with natural sweetness from dates and apples. Incidentally, the recipe is a "success always" recipe: Nothing can go wrong here and it always tastes WOW.

Sugar-Free WOW Apple Cake

Makes:
8 Pieces

Prep Time:
25 Minutes
Cook Time:
60 Minutes

Ingredients

- 4 medium apples, peeled, cored, and sliced into thin slices
- 1 ½ cups + 1 tbsp all-purpose flour
- 1 tbsp cinnamon
- 1 tsp baking soda
- 1 cup soft dates such as Medjool or Deglet Noor
- 1 cup carbonated water
- ¾ cup water
- ½ cup coconut oil
- ⅓ cup almond slivers

Directions

1. Preheat the oven to 350 degrees F and grease a 9-inch round baking pan.
2. Peel and core the apples and slice them into thin slices. Set aside.
3. Mix the flour, cinnamon, and baking soda in a large bowl.
4. Add the dates, carbonated water, water, and coconut oil into a blender and blend on high speed until smooth. Pour the liquid ingredients into the bowl with the dry ingredients and use a spoon to mix and combine until smooth.
5. Fold the apples into the batter.

6. Pour the batter into the baking pan and spread it out evenly. Sprinkle the almond slivers on top and bake for 1 hour or until a toothpick inserted comes out clean.

Fudgy Brownies

19	**Nutrition Info Per Serving:** 64g Carbs, 5g Protein, 22g Fat, 468 Calories

Our Fudgy Brownies are an ooey gooey treat. They're made with real melted dark chocolate and cocoa powder to give you a rich, chewy brownie, just like you remember!

Fudgy Brownies

Makes:
9 Large Brownies

Prep Time:
15 Minutes
Cook Time:
35-40 Minutes

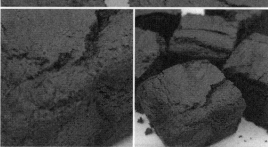

Ingredients

- 1 ½ cups all-purpose flour
- 1 tsp baking powder
- 1 tsp baking soda
- 1 ¼ cups coconut sugar
- 1 tbsp cocoa powder, unsweetened
- ½ tsp cinnamon
- Pinch of salt
- 1 cup non-dairy milk, unsweetened (e.g. almond milk)
- 5 tbsp vegan butter
- 1 ½ cups dark chocolate

Directions

1. Preheat the oven to 350 degrees F. Line a 9x9-inch square baking pan with parchment paper and set aside.
2. In a large bowl, whisk together the flour, baking powder, baking soda, coconut sugar, cocoa powder, cinnamon, and salt.
3. Add the milk to the dry ingredients and whisk to combine.
4. In a double boiler, melt the vegan butter. When the butter is just melted, add the dark chocolate and stir until melted.
5. Pour the chocolate mixture into the batter and whisk until just combined.

Do not over stir.
6. Pour the batter into the baking pan and bake for 35-40 minutes, or until a toothpick inserted comes out clean.
7. Cool completely, slice, and serve!

Cinnamon Sugar Donuts

20	**Nutrition Info Per Serving:** 32g Carbs, 3g Protein, 7g Fat, 216 Calories

This is another recipe that's our top favorite! Sink your teeth into these donuts and let the cinnamon transport you back to childhood. But don't be fooled by the taste – these babies are healthy! Not only do they contain oats and chia seeds, but they're baked instead of fried.

Dessert Idea for Donut Day (every first Friday of June)

Ingredients

- ¾ cup oat flour
- ¼ cup chia seeds
- 1 tbsp cinnamon
- 1 ½ tsp baking powder
- ½ cup maple syrup
- ¼ cup non-dairy milk, unsweetened (e.g. almond milk)
- 1 tsp vanilla extract
- Coconut oil, for greasing the pan and brushing the donuts
- 3 tbsp cane sugar for coating
- 1 tbsp cinnamon for coating

Directions

1. Preheat your oven to 325 degrees F.
2. If you need to make your oat flour, grind a ¾ cup of dried large flake oats in your blender until fine.
3. Sift your oat flour, baking powder, and cinnamon in a medium bowl. Add the chia seeds, whisk together, and set aside.
4. In a small bowl, whisk together maple syrup, non-dairy milk, and vanilla.
5. Add the wet ingredients to the dry ingredients and whisk until smooth. Do not let this mixture sit for too long because you don't want the chia seeds to expand.
6. Grease your donut pan with just a little bit of coconut oil. You don't need too much.
7. Distribute the batter evenly in the donut pan. Bake for 15-18 minutes, or until a toothpick inserted comes out clean.
8. Allow the donuts to cool in the pan for 10 minutes. Remove them and allow them to cool completely.

Darling Recipe, Low-Fat

Cinnamon Sugar Donuts

Makes:
6 Donuts

Prep Time:
15 Minutes
Cook Time:
15-18 Minutes

9. When the donuts are completely cooled, whisk together the cane sugar and cinnamon in a small, shallow bowl.
10. Brush a small amount of melted coconut oil on all sides of each donut. Dip the donuts in the cinnamon sugar and coat completely. Serve and enjoy!

Glazed Chocolate Donuts

| 21 | **Nutrition Info Per Serving:** 42g Carbs, 3g Protein, 8g Fat, 251 Calories |

Moist, cakey, sweet, and perfectly glazed: Our baked, chocolatey donuts are perfectly reminiscent of the classic donuts you find in a donut shop. They are coated with a sugar glaze on which you can stick colorful toppings (sugar sprinkles, coconut flakes, or chopped almonds, etc.) – or enjoy them as is. Yummy!

Dessert Idea for Donut Day (every first Friday of June)

Ingredients

Batter

- 1 tbsp flax meal
- 3 tbsp water
- ¾ cup all-purpose flour
- ¼ cup cocoa powder, unsweetened
- ½ tsp baking powder
- ¼ tsp baking soda
- ½ cup cane sugar
- ½ cup non-dairy milk, unsweetened (e.g. almond milk)
- 3 tbsp coconut oil, melted
- 1 tsp vanilla extract

Glaze

- ½ cup powdered cane sugar
- 1 tbsp non-dairy milk, unsweetened
- Optional: decoration such as pistachios, sugar sprinkles, coconut flakes, chopped almonds

Directions

1. Preheat the oven to 375 degrees F. Grease a 6 mold donut tin with a bit of coconut oil and set aside.
2. In a small bowl whisk together the flax meal and water and set aside for at least 10 min.
3. In a large bowl mix the flour, cocoa powder, baking powder, baking soda, and cane sugar until combined.
4. Add the milk, melted coconut oil, and vanilla to the bowl and mix to combine.
5. Distribute the batter between the 6 donut molds and bake for 10 minutes, ensuring a toothpick inserted comes out clean.

Glazed Chocolate Donuts

Makes:
6 Donuts

Prep Time:
15 Minutes
Cook Time:
10 Minutes

6. While the donuts are cooling, make your glaze by whisking together the powdered sugar and milk until smooth. Dip the donuts in the glaze when they are cooled, add decoration, and allow the glaze to harden before serving. Enjoy!

Red Velvet Donuts

| 22 | **Nutrition Info Per Serving:** 40g Carbs, 6g Protein, 8g Fat, 264 Calories |

The secret to the gorgeous red color in these red velvet donuts? Beet juice! You don't need to use artificial colors when mother nature provides beautiful colors and flavors for you!

Dessert Idea for Donut Day

Ingredients

Batter
- ¾ cup oat flour
- ¼ cup chia seeds
- 2 tbsp cocoa powder
- 1 ½ tsp baking powder
- ¼ cup non-dairy milk, unsweetened (e.g. almond milk)
- ½ cup maple syrup
- 3 tbsp beet juice
- 1 tsp vanilla extract

Icing
- ½ cup cashews (soak for a few hours if you don't have a powerful blender)
- ⅓ cup cold water
- ¼ cup maple syrup
- 1 tbsp lemon juice
- ½ tsp vanilla extract 1 tbsp lemon zest
- 1 tsp vanilla extract

Directions

1. Preheat the oven to 315 degrees F. Grease a 6 cavity donut tray with a very small amount of coconut oil and set aside.
2. Sift the flour into a medium sized bowl. Add the chia seeds, cocoa powder, and baking powder and whisk to combine.
3. In a small bowl whisk together the milk, beet juice, maple syrup, and vanilla extract.
4. Combine the dry ingredients with the wet ingredients and stir to combine.
5. Pour the batter into the donut mold and distribute equally between the 6 cavities.
6. Bake for about 18 minutes, or until a tooth-pick inserted comes out clean.
7. Remove the donuts from the oven and allow

Red Velvet Donuts

Makes:
6 Donuts

Prep Time:
15 Minutes
Cook Time:
18 Minutes

to cool. Make your icing by blending all of the icing ingredients on high speed until smooth. Set aside in the fridge.

8. When the donuts are completely cooled, remove the icing from the fridge and dip the donuts in the icing to coat the top. You can dip them a few times to get a few layers. Enjoy!

Lemon Donuts

| 23 | **Nutrition Info Per Serving:** 33g Carbs, 3g Protein, 3g Fat, 182 Calories |

Every first Friday of June is National Donut Day. Who said donuts can't be healthy? Say hello to delicious donuts that are low-fat. Wow! Chia seeds is the secret ingredient in this recipe that makes them super fluffy and delicious.

Dessert Idea for Donut Day (every first Friday of June)

LemonDonuts

 Makes:
6 Donuts

 Prep Time:
10 Minutes
Cook Time:
18-20 Minutes

Ingredients

Batter

- ¾ cup oat flour
- ¼ cup chia seeds
- 1 ½ tsp baking powder
- ½ cup maple syrup
- ¼ cup non-dairy milk, unsweetened (e.g. almond milk)
- 2 tbsp lemon juice
- Zest of one lemon
- 1 tsp vanilla extract

Glaze

- ¼ cup powdered cane sugar
- 2 tsp water
- 1 tsp lemon juice

Directions

1. Preheat the oven to 325 degrees F. Grease a 6 section donut pan with a bit of coconut oil. Do not over grease.
2. In a medium bowl, whisk together the oat flour, chia seeds, and baking powder. If you don't have oat flour, you can easily make it by putting oats in the blender until it is a fine powder.
3. In a small bowl, whisk together maple syrup, milk, lemon juice, lemon zest, and vanilla.
4. Combine the wet and dry ingredients until just combined. Distribute the batter between the 6 donut molds. Bake for 18-20 min, or until a toothpick inserted comes out clean.

5. When the donuts are cooled, make your icing by whisking together the powdered sugar, water, and lemon juice until smooth. Drizzle the icing on the donuts and garnish with additional lemon zest.

Hazelnut Bundt Cake

24   **Nutrition Info Per Serving:** 37g Carbs, 4g Protein, 12g Fat, 244 Calories

Here's a favorite fast and super simple cake recipe. Go nuts over this gorgeous Hazelnut Bundt Cake! The cake smells of toasted hazelnuts and has a sweet, rich flavor. It pairs perfectly with a cup of tea or coffee on a Sunday afternoon with friends.

Hazelnut Bundt Cake

Makes:
10 Servings

Prep Time:
20 Minutes
Cook Time:
50 Minutes

Ingredients

- 1 ¾ cups ground hazelnuts
- 1 ½ cups all-purpose flour
- 1 cup cane sugar
- 1 ½ tsp baking powder
- Pinch of salt
- 1 cup non-dairy milk, unsweetened (e.g. almond milk)
- 1 tsp vanilla extract
- Powdered cane sugar for coating

Directions

1. Preheat the oven to 350 degrees F and grease a Bundt cake pan with coconut oil.
2. In a large bowl, whisk together the ground hazelnuts, flour, cane sugar, baking powder, and salt until mixed.
3. Add the milk and vanilla and stir to combine. Do not overmix.
4. Pour the batter into the cake pan. Bake for 50 minutes, or until a toothpick inserted comes out clean. Allow it to cool completely before removing from the pan.
5. When the cake is cooled, remove it from the pan and dust it with powdered cane sugar. Slice, serve, and enjoy!

Chocolate Chip Pumpkin Loaf

25 | **Nutrition Info Per Serving:** 40g Carbs, 3g Protein, 9g Fat, 254 Calories

Pumpkin spice and everything nice, is this Pumpkin Loaf! This loaf is moist, chocolatey, and perfectly spiced! You can also make this recipe into muffins and just reduce the cooking time. so moist and healthy too!

Ingredients

- 1 ¾ cups all-purpose flour
- ½ cup cane sugar
- ¼ cup coconut sugar
- 2 ½ tsp baking powder
- ¼ tsp baking soda
- Pinch of salt
- 2 tsp cinnamon
- ½ tsp ginger
- ½ tsp allspice
- ¼ tsp nutmeg
- 1 cup canned pumpkin purée*
- ½ cup non-dairy milk, unsweetened
- ¼ cup coconut oil, melted
- 1 tbsp maple syrup
- ¼ cup mini chocolate chips
  + a few tsp for topping

Directions

1. Preheat the oven to 350 degrees F and line a loaf pan with parchment paper.
2. In a medium bowl, whisk together the flour, cane sugar, coconut sugar, baking powder, baking soda, spices, and salt. Set aside.
3. In another medium bowl, whisk together pumpkin, milk, coconut oil, and maple syrup.
4. Add the wet ingredients to the dry and stir to combine. Add ¼ cup of chocolate chips and stir again.
5. Pour the batter into the pan and bake for 60 minutes, or until a toothpick inserted comes out clean.
6. Allow the loaf to cool completely before slicing. Slice and serve!

Darling Recipe

Chocolate Chip Pumpkin Loaf

Makes:
10 Slices

Prep Time:
15 Minutes
Cook Time:
60 Minutes

* It is easy to make pumpkin purée from scratch. You have two options:

In the oven: Wash a Hokkaido pumpkin and cut in half (do not peel!). Remove the insides. Place the pumpkin halves with the cut side down on a baking sheet lined with baking paper. Bake at 350°F until a fork can easily pierce the pumpkin (about 1 to 1 ½ h). Remove from the oven, allow to cool, and puree with a little water.

In water: Wash a Hokkaido pumpkin and cut into pieces (do not peel!). Remove the insides. Cook in boiling water until the pumpkin is soft (about 20 minutes). Then dump the water and purée everything until it is the consistency of apple sauce.

Halloween Cupcakes

| 26 | **Nutrition Info Per Serving:** 36g Carbs, 2g Protein, 18g Fat, 307 Calories |

Spooktacularly yummy - We'll admit, our little vegan ghosts aren't especially scary, but they are pretty delicious. We know they are sugar bombs, but for that exact reason, they also have that special soul comforting quality we need. If this monster cupcake is too sweet for you, just omit the topping, which also has the lion's share of sugar. Then all that's left are the chocolate cupcakes. Their intense cocoa taste could hardly be any better!

Dessert Idea for Halloween

Ingredients

Batter

- 1 ¼ cups flour
- ⅔ cup brown sugar
- 2 tsp baking powder
  (instead of 2 tsp baking powder, you could use 1 tsp baking soda and 1 tsp citric acid)
- 3 tbsp vegan cocoa
- ¼ cup neutral oil
- 1 cup mineral or flat water

Topping

- 1 cup vegan margarine
- 2 cups powdered sugar
  (vegan powdered sugar from raw sugar)
- 1 tsp grated orange or lemon rind, untreated
- Vegan chocolate chips, for decorating

Directions

1. Preheat the oven to 350 degrees F
   (or 320 degrees F for convection ovens).
2. For the topping, sift the powdered sugar on top of the margarine. Beat with an electric mixer until creamy and the powdered sugar is completely dissolved. Add orange rind and mix well. Put the bowl of frosting in the refrigerator until needed.
3. Mix flour, baking powder, and cocoa together and then sift into a bowl. Add the sugar, mixing well with a fork. Gradually add oil and water, mixing with a fork or whisk. You should have a thick batter that drips slowly from your fork or whisk.

Darling Recipe

Halloween Cupcakes

Makes:
12 Cupcakes

Prep Time:
20 Minutes
Cook Time:
15 Minutes

4. Place cupcake cups in a cupcake pan and fill with batter. Each cup should be about ⅔ full. Bake for 15 minutes at 350 degrees F (or 320 F for convection ovens). The cupcakes are done when an inserted toothpick comes out clean. Leave to cool.
5. When the cupcakes are cool, put the icing in the icing bag and pipe a ghost onto the cupcakes. Use chocolate chips to make eyes on the ghosts. Refrigerate until serving.

Serving tips:
Crumble the removed bits of cupcake. Sprinkle over the cupcakes. You can use the rest as scary, but edible, "grave earth" around the base of the cupcakes.
If you really want to be perfect, you can make the following chocolate tombstones: Break dark chocolate into pieces roughly the shape of tombstones. Don't worry if they are a little irregular. Pour melted white chocolate into a freezer bag and write on the tombstones. Leave to dry.

Chocoholic BundtCake

27   **Nutrition Info Per Serving:** 47g Carbs, 3g Protein, 10g Fat, 290 Calories

This cake is so incredible that no one even knows it's vegan. For an added touch, pair it with a cup of tea or a mug of coffee. It's a great dish to make when hosting a gathering. Or you can just eat the entire thing yourself. Nothing's wrong with that!

Ingredients

Batter

- 1 ¼ cups all-purpose flour, plus extra for dusting your pan
- ⅓ cup cocoa powder, unsweetened
- 1 tsp baking soda
- Pinch of salt
- 1 cup warm water
- 1 cup cane sugar
- ⅓ cup vegan butter, melted, plus extra for greasing your pan
- 1 tsp lemon juice
- 1 tsp vanilla extract

Icing

- ¼ cup vegan butter, unsalted if possible
- ⅓ cup powdered cane sugar
- 2 tbsp cocoa powder, unsweetened
- 1 tsp vanilla extract

Directions

1. Preheat oven to 350 degrees F. Grease your Bundt cake pan with about 1 tbsp vegan butter. Add a few spoons of flour into the pan and tip the pan from side to side to distribute the flour and coat the pan evenly.
2. In a medium bowl, sift together the flour, cocoa powder, baking soda, and salt. Whisk to combine and set aside.
3. In another medium bowl, combine the water, butter, sugar, lemon juice, and vanilla. Whisk together until smooth.
4. Add the wet ingredients to the dry and whisk until combined.
5. Pour the batter into the Bundt cake pan. Bake for 35-40 minutes, or until a toothpick inserted comes out clean.
6. Allow the cake to cool in the pan for at least

Chocoholic Bundt Cake

Makes:
1 Bundt Cake

Prep Time:
30 Minutes
Cook Time:
35-40 Minutes

20 minutes. When it is cool enough to remove, allow it to cool further.
7. When the cake is fully cooled, make your icing. Melt the butter in a saucepot. Add the rest of the icing ingredients and whisk until smooth and all of the sugar is dissolved. Slice and serve.

Traditional Waffles

Makes:
4-5 Waffles

Prep Time:
10 Minutes
Cook Time:
5 Minutes

Ingredients

- 1 ¼ cups non-dairy milk, unsweetened (e.g. almond milk)
- 1 tsp apple cider vinegar
- ¼ cup maple syrup
- ¼ cup coconut oil, melted
- 1 tsp vanilla extract
- 2 cups all-purpose flour
- 1 ½ tsp baking powder
- 1 tsp cinnamon
- ½ cup chocolate chips (optional)

Directions

1. In a medium bowl, whisk together the milk and apple cider vinegar and let it sit for 5 minutes.
2. Add the maple syrup, coconut oil, and vanilla extract. Stir to combine and set aside.
3. In another medium bowl, whisk together the flour, baking powder, and cinnamon.
4. Add the liquid to the dry ingredients and whisk to combine. If you're making chocolate chip waffles, add the chocolate chips and stir.
5. Heat your waffle iron and gently grease it with a small amount of coconut oil. When the iron is heated, add the batter. This batter is thick, and you'll want to add enough to

 evenly spread across the waffle iron. Cook the waffles until they are fully baked. Cooking time can vary for each waffle iron, so follow the instructions for your iron.
6. Serve with maple syrup, fruit, or cinnamon, etc.

Carrot Cake Muffins

Nutrition Info Per Serving: 20g Carbs, 2g Protein, 1g Fat, 107 Calories

A particularly tasty recipe that will sweeten the Easter brunch for you and your family. It's made of healthy ingredients, such as oats, carrots, and raisins, and is naturally sweetened with dates and banana. The muffins are quickly stirred together and you are absolutely assured of success – and not just for carrot cake lovers.

Dessert Idea for Easter

Low-Fat

Carrot Cake Muffins

Makes:
12 Servings

Prep Time:
20 Minutes
Cook Time:
30 Minutes

Ingredients

- 1 ¾ cups oats or oat flour
- 2 tsp baking powder
- 1 tsp baking soda
- 2 tsp cinnamon
- 1 tsp allspice
- 1 ½ cups non-dairy milk, unsweetened (e.g. almond milk)
- 12 soft dates such as Deglet Noor, or 6-7 Medjool dates
- ½ ripe banana
- ¼ cup raisins
- 1 tsp vanilla extract
- 1 ½ cups carrots, shredded
- ½ cup raisins

Directions

1. Preheat your oven to 350 degrees F and line a 12 cup muffin pan with muffin liners. Set aside.
2. If you don't have oat flour, grind oats in a blender until fine. If you do, skip this step. Combine the flour with the baking powder, baking soda, cinnamon, and allspice. Set aside.
3. In a high-powered blender, blend the milk, dates, banana, ¼ cup raisins, and vanilla until very smooth and well-combined.
4. Add the wet ingredients to the dry ingredients and whisk to combine.

5. Add the shredded carrot and remaining raisins to the mixture and fold to combine.
6. Divide the batter into the 12 muffin cups and bake for 30 minutes, or until a toothpick inserted comes out clean. Allow to cool before serving.

Cinnamon Granola

| 35 | **Nutrition Info Per Serving:** 37g Carbs, 12g Protein, 26g Fat, 441 Calories |

Granola is crispy baked muesli and one of the most popular breakfast meals. The base is made from oatmeal, nuts, and dates, so you could eat it for breakfast or a snack.

P.S. This granola can be used as a topping for many desserts. We love it on ice cream – ohhhsogiganticlydelicious...

Cinnamon Granola

Makes:
5 Servings

Prep Time:
10 Minutes
Cook Time:
30 Minutes

Ingredients

- 2 cups rolled oats
- 1 ½ cups mixed nuts, chopped (almonds, hazelnuts, pecans, walnuts, etc.)
- 3 tbsp cinnamon
- Pinch of salt
- ¾ cup dates
- ¾ cup water
- 2 tbsp almond butter
- 1 tsp vanilla extract

Directions

1. Preheat your oven to 325 degrees F. Line a baking sheet with parchment and set aside.
2. In a medium bowl add the oats, nuts, cinnamon, and salt, and stir to combine.
3. In a blender, blend together the dates, water, almond butter, and vanilla until smooth.
4. Add the liquid to the dry ingredients and mix until well coated and combined.
5. Pour the granola onto a parchment lined baking sheet and spread out evenly. Bake for 30 minutes.
6. When the granola is cooled, break it apart into pieces and store in an airtight container.

Strawberry Whipped Cream Crêpes

36	**Nutrition Info Per Serving:** 71g Carbs, 9g Protein, 23g Fat, 564 Calories

The French classic crêpes come in all forms and flavors, but sweet crêpes are among the most commonly prepared variations. Fresh, juicy strawberries and our delicious vegan "whipped cream" recipe come together to make a heavenly combination – and an incredible dessert, breakfast, or brunch.

Ingredients

Crêpe Batter
- 1 ½ cups all-purpose flour
- 1 tbsp cane sugar
- ½ tsp baking powder
- Pinch of salt
- 2 tbsp coconut oil, plus more for pan-greasing
- 2 cups non-dairy milk, unsweetened
- ½ tsp vanilla extract

Whipped Cream
- 2 15 oz. cans full fat coconut milk, chilled
- ¼ cup maple syrup
- 1 tsp vanilla extract

Strawberry Compote
- 3 cups frozen strawberries
- 1 tbsp maple syrup

Powdered cane sugar for garnish

Directions

1. In a large bowl, whisk together the flour, sugar, baking powder, and salt. Set aside.
2. In a small pot, gently heat the milk and oil until the oil is melted. Whisk everything to combine.
3. Add the liquid and the vanilla extract to the dry ingredients and whisk together until combined.
4. Heat a large non-stick pan on medium heat and use a brush tool to spread a generous amount of coconut oil on the pan.
5. When the pan is hot enough, add approximately 1 ladle full of batter onto the pan and spread it out evenly. Cook for approximately 5 minutes on each side. Set the crêpe aside on a plate and repeat with the rest of the batter. You will have approximately 6 crêpes in total.

Strawberry Whipped Cream Crêpes

Makes:
3 Servings (6 Crêpes)

Prep Time:
30 Minutes
Cook Time:
10 Minutes Per Crepe

6. When the crêpes are all cooked, set them aside to allow them to cool slightly. While the crêpes are cooling, make the whipped cream. Remove the 2 cans of coconut milk from the fridge and turn them upside down. Open each can. There will be coconut water on top. Pour this out into a bowl as you won't need it for this recipe.
7. Now at the bottom of the cans there will be very thick coconut cream. Add this cream to the bowl of a stand mixer. Add the maple syrup and vanilla and mix on medium/high speed until it becomes a nice and fluffy whipped cream. This will take 5-10 minutes.
8. Make your compote by cooking strawberries and maple syrup for about 5 minutes on medium heat.
9. Now you can assemble your crepes. Fill with a few spoons of whipped cream and strawberries and fold over. Garnish with additional cream and strawberries. Sift a small amount of powdered cane sugar on top. Serve and enjoy!

Spiced Apple Muffins

37	**Nutrition Info Per Serving:** 12g Carbs, 7g Protein, 10g Fat, 167 Calories

The Spiced Apple Muffins are the perfect dessert for those who like to eat a healthy, low-fat dessert. This variety is gluten-free, high in protein & fiber, and low in sugar. Just bake and enjoy!

Gluten-Free, Low-Fat, Easy

Spiced Apple Muffins

Makes:
10 Muffins

Prep Time:
20 Minutes
Cook Time:
25-30 Minutes

Ingredients

- ½ cup almond flour
- ½ cup vegan vanilla protein powder
- 1 tsp baking powder
- 1 tbsp cinnamon
- ¼ tsp nutmeg
- ¼ tsp cloves
- 1 cup apple sauce, unsweetened
- ½ cup almond butter
- ⅓ cup maple syrup

Directions

1. Preheat the oven to 350 degrees F and grease 10 cavities of a muffin tin with coconut oil.
2. In a medium bowl, sift together the almond flour, protein powder, baking powder, and spices.
3. In another medium bowl, whisk together the apple sauce, almond butter, and maple syrup.
4. Add the liquid to the dry ingredients and mix until well combined.
5. Bake the muffins for 25-30 minutes, or until a toothpick inserted comes out clean. Allow the muffins to cool before serving.

Chapter 4

Tarts, Pies, and Pastries

Is your platter feeling lonely? Then bake up some tarts, pies, and pastries. Whether you're hosting a party or just want some treats on hand in case you're hungry, these are the perfect accessory for your kitchen.

Chocolate Tartlets

| 38 | **Nutrition Info Per Serving:** 52g Carbs, 4g Protein, 31g Fat, 510 Calories |

An adorable dessert for special occasions are our chocolate tartlets. Your gourmet guests won't be able to resist this sweet little tartlet, made of delicious, soft dough with a creamy chocolate pudding filling and a fresh blackberry. They are prepared in 25 minutes or less and will look fabulous on the dessert table.

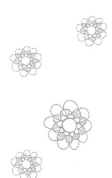

Chocolate Tartlets

Makes:
4 Tartlets

Prep Time:
15 Minutes
Cook Time:
10 Minutes

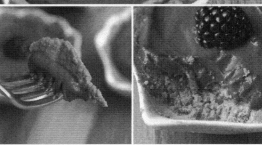

Ingredients

Crust
- 240g vegan graham cracker crumbs
- ¼ cup coconut oil, melted

Chocolate Pudding
- 1 large ripe avocado
- ¼ cup + 2 tbsp cocoa powder
- ¼ cup non-dairy milk, unsweetened (e.g. almond milk)
- 2 tbsp maple syrup
- ½ tsp vanilla extract

4 blackberries (or other berries) for topping

Directions

1. Preheat the oven to 350 degrees F.
2. In a medium bowl, combine the graham cracker crumbs with melted coconut oil. Alternatively, you can also blend graham crackers in a food processor and blend in the melted coconut oil.
3. Grease 4 shallow tart pans with coconut oil. Distribute the graham crumbs between the 4 pans and spread the crumbs evenly to form a crust.
4. Bake the crusts for 10 minutes.
5. While the crust is baking, make the chocolate filling by blending all of the pudding ingredients in a blender until smooth.
6. Remove the pans and allow the crust to cool.
7. Pour the pudding into each crust and distribute evenly.
8. Top with 1 blackberry and serve immediately or chill in the fridge.

Strawberry Shortcake

39   **Nutrition Info Per Serving:** 52g Carbs, 3g Protein, 13g Fat, 350 Calories

Take a stroll down memory lane with this strawberry shortcake recipe – another favorite. It'll take you back to the days when you were licking whipped cream off the spoon. It's a perfect dish to bring to a party or hog all to yourself. The second option might be better.

Ingredients

Batter
- 1 ¼ cups all-purpose flour
- 1 tsp baking soda
- Pinch of salt
- 1 cup warm water
- 1 cup cane sugar
- ⅓ cup vegan butter, melted, plus extra for greasing your pan
- 1 tsp lemon juice
- 1 tsp vanilla extract

Icing
- The cream from 1 14 oz can of full fat coconut milk, chilled in the fridge overnight
- 3 tbsp maple syrup
- ½ tsp vanilla extract
- ¾ cup strawberries, diced into small chunks
- Additional strawberries for decorating

Directions

1. Preheat your oven to 350 degrees F. Grease a round 9-inch baking pan with vegan butter.
2. In a medium bowl, sift together the flour, baking soda, and salt. Whisk to combine.
3. In another medium bowl, combine the water, butter, sugar, lemon juice, and vanilla. Whisk together until smooth.
4. Add the wet to the dry ingredients and whisk until combined.
5. Pour the batter into the pan and bake for 40-45 minutes, or until a toothpick comes out clean.
6. Allow the cake to cool completely.
7. When the cake is cooled, make your whipped cream icing. Take your canned coconut milk out of the fridge and turn it upside down. When you open the can, the coconut water should be on top and the cream should be on

Makes:
8 Servings

Prep Time:
20 Minutes
Cook Time:
40-45 Minutes

the bottom. Pour out the coconut water, as you don't need it for this recipe. You can save it to drink, or add to smoothies, etc…

8. Scoop out the cream from the can and pour it into the bowl of a stand mixer. Add the maple syrup and vanilla and beat on medium-high speed for about 10 minutes, until the mixture becomes nice and fluffy.
9. Chop up your fresh strawberries into small chunks. Add to the whipped cream and beat for another 2 minutes, until the whipped cream turns pink.
10. Pour all of the icing on top of the cake and distribute evenly. Top with additional fresh strawberry slices for garnish. Alternatively, you can cut the cake in half to create two thin layers, then add the whipped strawberry cream on top of one layer. Add the second cake layer on top and spread the additional whipped cream and distribute evenly. Garnish with additional fresh strawberries. Chill in the fridge until serving.

Pecan Pie

40 | **Nutrition Info Per Serving:** 52g Carbs, 4g Protein, 34g Fat, 536 Calories

This classic Southern treat will test your patience while you're waiting for it to cool! The Pecan Pie smells incredible coming out of the oven. It tastes caramelly, nutty, flaky, and buttery (it's impossible to go wrong with that!) and is mostly served on holidays.

Dessert Idea for Christmas/Thanksgiving

Ingredients

Crust

- 1 ½ cups all-purpose flour
- ¼ tsp salt
- ½ cup coconut oil
- 4-5 tbsp ice water

Filling

- 2 tbsp ground flax
- ¼ cup + 2 tbsp water
- ½ cup coconut sugar
- ¼ cup cane sugar
- 3 tbsp corn starch (or tapioca, arrowroot, etc.)
- ½ tsp cinnamon
- ½ cup maple syrup
- ¼ cup non-dairy milk, unsweetened
- ¼ cup vegan butter, melted
- 1 tsp vanilla extract
- 1 ¼ cups pecans

Directions

1. Begin by making your pie crust. In a large bowl, mix together the flour and salt.
2. Add the coconut oil and use your hands to cut it into the flour. It will look a bit crumbly.
3. Add the water and mix to form a dough. If the dough is too crumbly, add a bit more water 1 tsp at a time.
4. When the dough is smooth, form a dough ball and roll it out onto a large surface until it is large enough for your 9-inch pie pan. You do not need to refrigerate this dough.
5. Place the crust into the pie pan and pinch the rim of the pan to form nice edges. Cut off any excess dough.
6. Preheat the oven to 350 degrees F.
7. In a small bowl, whisk together the ground flax and water. Set aside for around 10 minutes.

Pecan Pie

Makes:
One 9-inch Pie

Prep Time:
25 Minutes
Cook Time:
50 Minutes

8. In a medium bowl, add the coconut and cane sugar, corn starch, cinnamon.
9. In another bowl, whisk together the maple syrup, non-dairy milk, melted butter, and vanilla extract.
10. Add the wet ingredients to the dry ingredients and mix until combined. Fold in the pecans.
11. Pour the filling into the pie crust. Bake for 25 minutes.
12. Reduce the heat to 275 degrees F and bake for another 25 minutes.
13. Remove the pie from the oven and allow it to cool completely before slicing.

Classic Pumpkin Pie

41	**Nutrition Info Per Serving:** 45g Carbs, 4g Protein, 11g Fat, 297 Calories

Healthy and delicious, this pumpkin pie recipe brings holiday cheer all year long. Make it in April or July or November. It's packed with a smooth pumpkin pie filling, laced with vanilla and cinnamon - yep, it's something you can truly be thankful for!

Dessert Idea for Thanksgiving

Ingredients

Crust
- 1 cup + 2 tbsp all-purpose flour
- 2 ½ tsp cane sugar
- ½ tsp salt
- ¼ cup solid coconut oil
- 3-4 tbsp cold water

Filling
- 1 14 oz can pumpkin pie filling* with pumpkin spices
- ¾ cup full fat coconut milk from a can
- ½ cup coconut sugar
- ¼ cup maple syrup
- ¼ cup tapioca starch
- 1 teaspoon vanilla extract
- ½ tsp cinnamon
- ¼ tsp salt

Directions

1. Preheat your oven to 350 degrees F.
2. Begin by making your crust. In a large bowl, sift and combine the flour, cane sugar, and salt.
3. Add the coconut oil and combine with your hands until it is crumbly but no oil clumps remain.
4. Add 3 tbsp of cold water into the dough and combine until a sticky dough forms. Add additional water if needed, 1 tbsp at a time.
5. Flour your work surface and a rolling pin. Roll the dough onto the surface and roll it out into a disk shape, large enough to fit your pie pan.
6. Place the dough in your pie pan and spread it out evenly, cutting off any excess trim. Set aside.
7. Now make your pie filling. In a medium bowl, whisk together all of the pie ingredients until smooth. Pour into your pie crust and bake for 50-60 minutes, or until the crust is golden.

Low-Fat

Classic Pumpkin Pie

Makes:
8 Servings

Prep Time:
25 Minutes

Cook Time:
50-60 Minutes

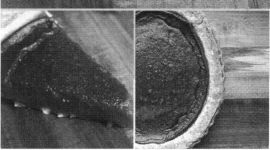

* Pumpkin pie filling from scratch:

Pumpkin spice for one standard pie
- 1 tsp cinnamon
- ¼ tsp nutmeg
- ¼ tsp ginger, and
- 1/8 tsp cloves

Directions: Preheat the oven to 350°F. Cut 1 Hokkaido pumpkin in half, lengthwise. Remove the seeds and the pulp. Cover each half with foil. Bake in the preheated oven, foil side up for about 1 hour, or until fork tender. Scrape the pumpkin meat from the shell and puree it in a blender. Strain to remove any remaining stringy pieces. Add the pumpkin spice and mix well.

Linzer Torte ♥

42   **Nutrition Info Per Serving:** 40g Carbs, 7g Protein, 29g Fat, 463 Calories

So good that it has to go behind bars! The Linzer Torte is a traditional Austrian cake with raspberry jam or "Ribiselgelee" (redcurrant jelly). Incidentally, this cake is considered the oldest known cake recipe in the world! The secret ingredient in our version is the almond flour, which develops a heavenly scent when baking, and tastes indescribably delicious – the raspberry and almond combination is to die for.

If you love this recipe, try the Linzer Cookies in Chapter 7 of this book.

Ingredients

- 2 cups ground almonds
- 1 ¼ cups all-purpose flour
- ¾ cup vegan butter, room temperature
- ½ cup cane sugar
- 1 tsp cinnamon
- 1 tsp vanilla extract
- 1 cup raspberry jam

Directions

1. Preheat the oven to 350 degrees F and grease a springform pan. Set aside.
2. Begin by making your dough. In a large bowl, add the ground almonds, flour, vegan butter, cane sugar, cinnamon, and vanilla. Mix by hand until a dough forms and everything is evenly combined. If it is just a bit moist, add a little bit of flour at a time to get a nicer consistency. Roll the dough into a ball and wrap it in plastic wrap. Set it in the fridge to chill for 30 minutes.
3. When the dough is chilled, cut ⅓ of the dough off, wrap it up, and put it back in the fridge. Roll out the remaining dough into a circle and lay it into the greased pan so it covers the bottom and also the sides. This dough can be difficult to work with. If you are having a hard time, you can just press the dough evenly into the bottom and sides of the pan.
4. Pour the jam into the pan and spread evenly.
5. Take the remaining dough from the fridge and roll it out. Cut strips to top the torte, or decorate as you desire.
6. Bake for 45 minutes. If the dough is browning too quickly, you can cover it with tinfoil about halfway through baking.

Darling Recipe

Linzer Torte

Makes:
8 Slices

Prep Time:
50 Minutes
Cook Time:
45 Minutes

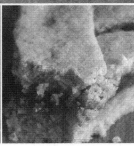

7. Allow the torte to cool completely before slicing. According to tradition, the cake should "rest" for a few days after baking so that the filling can pass through. But not everyone can wait that long... Enjoy!

Mini Strawberry Hearts

43 | **Nutrition Info Per Serving:** 21g Carbs, 2g Protein, 7g Fat, 154 Calories

Want a romantic dessert for your sweetheart? Cupid has his arrows, but you have seductive Strawberry Hearts. These mini pies are the perfect quick pleasure treats, which bring the taste of normal strawberry pies to the point! They are changeable, too. You can swap out the strawberry jam for blueberry or raspberry or cherry or ....

Dessert Idea for Valentine's Day

Ingredients

- 1 cup + 2 tbsp all-purpose flour
- 2 ½ tsp cane sugar
- ½ tsp salt
- ¼ cup solid coconut oil
- 3-4 tbsp cold water
- 8 tsp strawberry jam
- A few spoons of aquafaba (liquid from a can of chickpeas)
- Powdered cane sugar for sifting

Directions

1. Preheat your oven to 350 degrees F and line a small baking tray with parchment paper.
2. In a large bowl, sift and combine the flour, cane sugar, and salt.
3. Add the coconut oil and combine with your hands until it is crumbly but no oil clumps remain.
4. Add 3 tbsp of cold water into the dough and combine until a sticky dough forms. Add additional water if needed, 1 tbsp at a time.
5. Flour your work surface and a rolling pin. Roll the dough onto the surface and roll it until it is fairly thin.
6. Use a large heart shaped cookie cutter and cut out the pieces of dough (you should have about 16 in total).
7. Add 1 tsp of jam onto each of the 8 hearts.
8. Take the remaining hearts and sandwich them on top of the hearts with jam.

Mini Strawberry Hearts

Makes:
8 Mini Pies

Prep Time:
25 Minutes
Cook Time:
25 Minutes

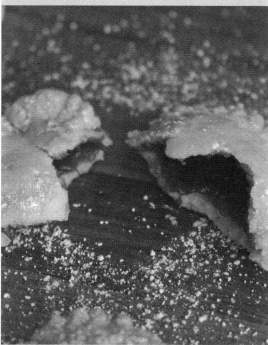

9. Use a fork to pinch the dough and seal all of the sides of each heart.
10. Gently brush the top and bottom of each heart with the aquafaba and place them on the baking tray.
11. Bake for 25 minutes. Sift powdered sugar on top of each heart. Enjoy!

Mini Pumpkin Tarts

44 | **Nutrition Info Per Serving:** 26g Carbs, 8g Protein, 17g Fat, 299 Calories

The perfect fall or holiday treat. They're the perfect last-minute dessert recipe. Perfectly spiced and sweetened, these single-serving-sized treats are a new, fun way to serve traditional pumpkin pies. Each guest will have their own delicious little pumpkin pie!

Dessert Idea for Thanksgiving/Christmas

Ingredients

Coconut oil for greasing

Crust
- 1 ½ cups almond flour
- 2 tbsp maple syrup
- 1 tbsp water

Filling
- 1 cup canned puréed pumpkin*
- ½ cup puréed baked sweet potato
- ¼ cup maple syrup
- 1 tsp cinnamon
- ¼ tsp nutmeg
- ¼ tsp ginger powder
- ¼ tsp allspice

Directions

1. Preheat the oven to 450 degrees F.
2. Wrap half of a medium peeled sweet potato in foil and bake until cooked – about 20 minutes. Poke holes in the potato for quicker baking.
3. Grease a muffin tin with coconut oil and cut strips of parchment to lay in the molds for easy removal. This recipe will make 5 tarts.
4. In a medium bowl, add the crust ingredients and mix until combined. Press the crust into 5 of the molds, spreading evenly onto the bottom and sides.
5. When the sweet potato is cooked, remove it from the oven and reduce the temperature to 375 degrees F. Blend all of the filling ingredients in a blender until smooth. Pour the filling into each cup and distribute evenly.
6. Bake for 30 minutes. Remove the tarts from the oven and allow them to cool. When the tarts are cool enough to remove, allow them to chill and set for at least 5 hours before serving.

Mini Pumpkin Tarts

Makes:
5 Tarts

Prep Time:
30 Minutes
Cook Time:
30 Minutes

* It is very easy to make pumpkin purée from scratch yourself.

You have two options:

In the oven: Wash a Hokkaido pumpkin and cut in half (do not peel!). Remove the insides (pumpkin seeds can be reserved for toasting). Place the pumpkin halves with the cut side down on a baking sheet lined with baking paper and bake at 350°F until a fork can easily pierce the pumpkin (about 1 to 1 ½ hours). Remove from the oven, allow to cool and puree with a little water.

In water: Wash a Hokkaido pumpkin and cut into pieces (do not peel!). Remove the insides. Cook in boiling water until the pumpkin is soft (about 20 minutes). Then dump the water and purée everything until it has the consistency of apple sauce.

Cherry Crumble

45	**Nutrition Info Per Serving:** 48g Carbs, 5g Protein, 20g Fat, 404 Calories

Crumble is a simple fruit dessert crowned with a crunchy, buttery crumble topping that turns every fruit into an irresistible dessert. Sweet, rich, buttery goodness - dark cherries paired with the crumble layers are a wonderful example of such a delicious treat.

Cherry Crumble

Makes:
9 Bars

Prep Time:
15 Minutes
Cook Time:
35 Minutes

Ingredients

- 3 cups all-purpose flour
- 1 cup vegan butter, room temperature
- ½ cup cane sugar
- 1 tsp vanilla extract
- 2 ½ cups fresh or frozen cherries

Directions

1. Preheat the oven to 350 degrees F and line a 9x9-inch square baking pan with parchment paper.
2. In a large bowl, combine all of the ingredients except for the cherries. Use your hands to combine the mixture evenly and create a crumbly dough. Take ⅔ of this mixture and press it evenly into the bottom of the pan.
3. Line the crust with the cherries.
   Fresh cherries are optimal, so that the juice doesn't bleed through to the crust when baked, but if you prefer to use pitted frozen cherries you can do that as well.
4. Top the cherries evenly with the rest of the crumble.
5. Bake for 35 minutes, or until the top layer turns golden brown.
6. Cool before slicing and enjoy!

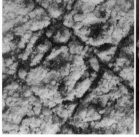

Flourless Peanut Butter Blondies

46 | **Nutrition Info Per Serving:** 22g Carbs, 8g Protein, 11g Fat, 226 Calories

A blondie is like an ooey gooey peanut butter brownie – also known as a blonde brownie. These are gluten-free and oil-free. They're made of chickpeas as a base, so they're completely flourless. Perfect to enjoy fresh out the oven with a glass of cold vanilla almond or soy milk.

Flourless Peanut Butter Blondies

Makes:
9 Blondies

Prep Time:
15 Minutes

Cook Time:
30 Minutes

Ingredients

- 1 15 oz can chickpeas, drained and rinsed
- ½ cup peanut butter, unsalted and unsweetened
- ¼ cup maple syrup
- ¼ cup coconut sugar
- 2 tbsp non-dairy milk, unsweetened (e.g. almond milk)
- 1 ½ tsp vanilla extract
- 1 tsp baking powder
- ¼ tsp baking soda
- Pinch of salt
- ¼ cup mini chocolate chips

Directions

1. Preheat your oven to 350 degrees F and line an 8x8-inch square baking pan with parchment.
2. Add all of the ingredients except for the chocolate chips into a high-powered blender and blend until smooth.
3. Scrape out all of the batter into the baking pan.
4. Add the chocolate chips to batter and gently stir them in to combine.
5. Bake for 30 minutes. Cool completely before slicing. Enjoy!

Apple Strudel

47   **Nutrition Info Per Serving:** 23g Carbs, 3g Protein, 8g Fat, 182 Calories

This traditional Austrian dessert will make your cooking skills look like that of a professional baker, but this delicious treat is actually quite easy to make. If you want to save more time in the kitchen while still fooling your friends and family into thinking you're a secret professional chef, use pre-made puff pastry dough instead.

Ingredients

Dough
- 1 ½ cups whole-wheat flour
- 1 ¼ cups all-purpose flour
- Pinch of salt
- ½ cup vegan butter
- 1 cup ice water
- 1 ½ tsp lemon juice

Filling
- 2 medium-sized, sweet apples
- 1 tbsp cinnamon
- 1 tbsp coconut sugar

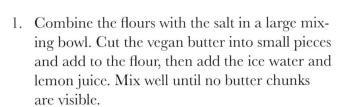

Directions

1. Combine the flours with the salt in a large mixing bowl. Cut the vegan butter into small pieces and add to the flour, then add the ice water and lemon juice. Mix well until no butter chunks are visible.
2. Dust a working surface (preferably wood) with some flour and turn the dough out on there. Knead for about a minute until the dough starts to come together.
3. Form a ball with the dough and put it back in a (floured) bowl. Cover with a tea towel, and refrigerate for two hours.
4. Preheat your oven to 350 degrees F.
5. A little while before the dough is ready to be removed from the fridge, slice up the apples into thin, uneven pieces. Add them to a mixing bowl and stir in the cinnamon and coconut sugar.
6. Turn out the dough on a floured working surface and roll it out into a large rectangular shape. Now evenly spread out the apple-cinnamon mixture over half of it.

Apple Strudel

 Makes:
4-5 Servings

 Prep Time:
2 Hours 10 Minutes (if making dough from scratch) or 9 Minutes (if using pre-made puff pastry)
Cook Time:
20 Minutes

7. Double the dough over, wrapping the apple-cinnamon mixture inside. Seal the edges by pressing them together.
8. Bake in the pre-heated oven for about 20 minutes. The top should be golden brown, the dough light and crunchy.
9. Hot or cold – it's delicious either way.

113

Coconut Layer Dream

48 | **Nutrition Info Per Serving:** 72g Carbs, 3g Protein, 27g Fat, 556 Calories

How about a short, decadent trip to the tropics? Our suggestion: A nutritious, soft and creamy, coconut-flavored cake that will satisfy your travel bug. This cake will send you to the tropics, but it's also perfect for an Easter holiday dessert with your loved ones.

Dessert Idea for Easter

Ingredients

Batter
- 1 15 oz can coconut milk
- 2 tsp apple cider vinegar
- 2 cups all-purpose flour
- 1 tsp baking powder
- ¾ tsp baking soda
- Pinch of salt
- 1 cup cane sugar
- ⅓ cup coconut oil, melted
- 1 tbsp vanilla extract

Frosting
- 1 cup coconut oil, room temperature
- 3 tbsp water
- 1 tsp vanilla extract
- 3 cups powdered cane sugar
- ½ cup toasted coconut flakes for garnish, unsweetened

Directions

1. Preheat your oven to 350 degrees F. Grease 2 9-inch circular baking pans with coconut oil. Trace the bottom of the pans onto parchment paper and cut 1 circle out to place on the bottom of each pan.
2. In a medium bowl, whisk together the coconut milk and apple cider vinegar. Allow it to sit for at least 5 minutes.
3. In a large bowl, add the flour, baking powder, baking soda, cane sugar, and salt and whisk it all together to combine.
4. Add the coconut oil and vanilla extract to the coconut milk and whisk.
5. Add the wet ingredients to the dry ingredients and stir to combine, but do not overmix.
6. Divide the cake batter in half and distribute the batter between the 2 cake pans evenly. Bake for 20-25 minutes or until cake is golden.

Coconut Layer Dream

Makes:
10 Servings

Prep Time:
25 Minutes

Cook Time:
20-25 Minutes

7. While the cake is baking, make the icing. In a stand mixer, cream the coconut oil with the water and vanilla extract for a few minutes. Add the powdered sugar and beat the mixture for at least 5 minutes, until fluffy.
8. When the cake is fully cooled, place one cake layer on a cake pedestal or a flat surface. Add half of the icing on top of this layer and spread it with a knife until it is spread evenly. Place the second cake layer on top and add the remaining icing to the top of the cake. Garnish with coconut flakes and refrigerate until serving.

Chapter 5

Spoon Desserts

Are you wondering if our desserts are truly irresistible? Then give this section a try. The proof is in this pudding! Grab a spoon and try not to swoon.

Sticky Toffee Pudding

49	**Nutrition Info Per Serving:** 37g Carbs, 2g Protein, 78g Fat, 226 Calories

Sweet, sticky, decadent – an absolute match made in heaven: Sticky Toffee Pudding is a classic English pudding made with delicious dates.
This dessert comes with a wonderfully sticky sauce that soaks the cupcake, and can be rounded off with a scoop of ice cream. No wonder it is one of Great Britain's favorites!

Ingredients

Batter

- ½ cup + 2 tbsp water, boiled
- 1 chai tea bag
- 1 cup soft dates
- ½ cup apple sauce, unsweetened
- ⅓ cup non-dairy milk, unsweetened (e.g. almond milk), room temperature
- ⅓ cup coconut oil, melted
- ⅓ cup cane sugar
- ¼ cup coconut sugar
- 1 tsp vanilla extract
- 1 cup + 1 tbsp all-purpose flour
- 1 tsp baking powder
- 1 tsp baking soda
- ½ tsp cinnamon

Sticky Toffee Sauce

- ½ cup coconut sugar
- ½ cup + 2 tbsp full fat coconut milk
- ¼ tsp vanilla extract
- Pinch of salt

Directions

1. Preheat the oven to 350 degrees F and grease 10 cavities of a muffin tin with coconut oil.
2. Boil the water, pour it in a glass with the chai tea bag, and let it steep for 10 minutes.
3. Remove the tea bag from the water and discard it. Pour the tea into a blender with the dates and blend until smooth. Set aside.
4. In a medium bowl, whisk together the apple sauce, milk, melted coconut oil, cane sugar, coconut sugar, and vanilla extract. If your almond milk isn't at room temperature, heat it up in the same pot when you are melting the coconut oil.

Darling Recipe

Sticky Toffee Pudding

Makes:
10 Servings

Prep Time:
20 Minutes
Cook Time:
30 Minutes

5. Add the date mixture to the bowl.
6. In a separate bowl, mix the flour, baking powder, baking soda, cinnamon.
7. Add the dry ingredients to the wet ingredients and mix to combine, but don't overmix.
8. Distribute the batter into the 10 muffin cavities and bake for 30 minutes.
9. While the batter is baking, make your sticky toffee sauce. In a small pot, whisk together the coconut sugar, vanilla, full fat coconut milk, and salt. Bring it to a gentle boil. Reduce the heat to low and cook for about 3 minutes, whisking.
10. Pour the pot into a glass container or bowl and if preferred, place it in the fridge (when it cools down it will become much thicker). Traditionally, the sauce is usually served warm.
11. Remove the cakes from the oven and allow them to cool completely before removing them from the pan.
12. Serve by plating with a generous drizzle of toffee sauce. Enjoy!

Vanilla Panna Cotta with Berry Sauce

50	**Nutrition Info Per Serving:** 31g Carbs, 1g Protein, 11g Fat, 241 Calories

Italy at its best: Panna Cotta is a Mediterranean dessert classic and is for good reason one of the most popular sweets in Europe. This elegant, creamy dessert is topped with a fresh-fruity berry sauce. The Vanilla Panna Cotta can be prepared simply and ahead of time and will definitely conjure up a touch of northern Italy on your table.

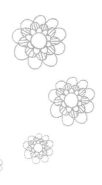

Vanilla Panna Cotta with Berry Sauce

Makes:
3 Servings

Prep Time:
10 Minutes
Chill Time:
4 Hours

Ingredients

Panna Cotta
- 1 15 oz can full fat coconut milk
- ¼ cup maple syrup
- 1 tsp vanilla extract
- 1 tsp agar powder

Berry Sauce
- ½ cup mixed berries, fresh or frozen
- 2 tbsp maple syrup

Directions

1. In a small saucepan add all of the ingredients except for the agar powder. Bring the mixture to a gentle boil and stir.
2. When the milk begins to boil, reduce the heat to medium and add the agar. Whisk the mixture for about 3 minutes and ensure it is gently bubbling the whole time. The milk will thicken slightly but not too much.
3. Pour the milk mixture into 3 ramekins. Allow them to chill until fully set – at least 4 hours.
4. When the mixture is completely set, make your berry sauce by heating the berries and syrup in a small saucepot. If you are using frozen berries, heat until the berries are thawed. If you are using fresh berries, heat until the berries break down slightly.
5. Remove the panna cotta from the ramekins. To do this, slide a knife around the edges and gently slide the knife underneath the panna cotta to release it from the mold.
6. Plate the panna cottas on plates, and add the berry sauce to the top of each one. Serve and enjoy!

121

Tiramisu

| 51 | **Nutrition Info Per Serving:** 189g Carbs, 24g Protein, 80g Fat, 1571 Calories |

One of the most popular desserts in the world and a popular Venetian classic, is Tiramisu. Three easy-to-make components make up this delightful trio of sponge cake, espresso cream, and chocolate sauce. Tiramisu is a dish that not only looks incredibly elegant, but tastes even better... especially served in a glass!

Ingredients

Sponge Cake
- 1 ½ cups all-purpose flour
- 1 tsp baking powder
- 1 tsp baking soda
- Pinch of salt
- 1 tsp cinnamon
- ⅔ cup water
- ½ cup brewed coffee
- ½ cup maple syrup
- ⅓ cup coconut oil, melted
- 2 tbsp apple cider vinegar
- 1 tsp vanilla extract

Espresso Cream
- 1 cup cashews
- ¼ cup + 2 tbsp brewed coffee
- ¼ cup maple syrup
- ½ tsp vanilla extract
- Pinch of salt

Chocolate Sauce
- ¼ cup cocoa powder, unsweetened
- 3 tbsp maple syrup
- 2 tbsp coconut oil

Cocoa powder for garnish

Directions

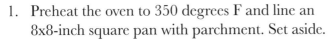

1. Preheat the oven to 350 degrees F and line an 8x8-inch square pan with parchment. Set aside.
2. In a large bowl add the flour, baking powder, baking soda, cinnamon, and salt, and whisk.
3. Add the water, coffee, maple syrup, melted coconut oil, apple cider vinegar, and vanilla. Whisk until smooth and combined.
4. Pour the batter into the baking pan and bake the sponge cake in the center rack of your oven for 25 minutes, or until a toothpick inserted comes out clean.
5. While the cake is baking, prepare the espresso cream by blending all of the ingredients in a

Tiramisu

Makes:
2 Large Servings

Prep Time:
25 Minutes
Cook Time:
25 Minutes

high-powered blender until smooth. Set aside in the fridge to chill.

6. Make the chocolate sauce by gently heating the ingredients in a small saucepan until the coconut oil is melted. Whisk until smooth.
7. When the sponge cake is finished, remove it from the oven and allow it to cool completely.
8. When the cake is fully cooled, take 2 large cups that you will be using for serving and use one of them to punch 4 holes out of the sponge cake. The leftover trimmings can be eaten separately if you don't want to discard them.
9. To layer the tiramisu, add 1 piece of sponge cake to the bottom of a cup. Pour in a ¼ of the espresso cream first, and then a ¼ of the chocolate sauce. Add a second piece of cake on top and pour in another quarter each of the espresso cream and chocolate sauce. Dust a small amount of cocoa powder on top for garnish. Repeat this with the second glass. Chill until serving.

Maple Vanilla Baked Pears

52	**Nutrition Info Per Serving:** 18g Carbs, 2g Protein, 5g Fat, 129 Calories

This is a perfect recipe for fall or winter. On a cold day, you can enjoy a warm, perfectly spiced and sweetened dessert, made with healthy ingredients.

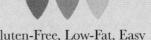

Gluten-Free, Low-Fat, Easy

Maple Vanilla Baked Pears

 Makes:
4 Servings

 Prep Time:
5 Minutes
Cook Time:
30 Minutes

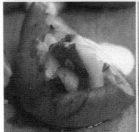
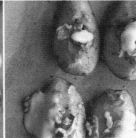

Ingredients

- 2 large ripe pears,
  such as D'Anjou or Bartlett
- 1 tbsp maple syrup
- ½ tsp cinnamon
- ¼ tsp vanilla extract
- ¼ cup walnuts
- Coconut yogurt for garnish
  (optional)

Directions

1. Preheat the oven to 350 degrees F and line a small baking tray with parchment. Set aside.
2. Cut the pears into quarters and remove the core and stems with a knife. Then use a spoon to scoop out any remaining seeds or core, and to make a small well in each pear. Line up each pear on the parchment with the skin down.
3. In a small bowl, whisk together the maple syrup, cinnamon, and vanilla. Drizzle the maple mixture evenly on each pear.
4. Chop the walnuts into small pieces and sprinkle them over the pears.
5. Bake for 30 minutes. Serve hot. When ready to serve, you can garnish them with a bit of coconut yogurt on top if desired. Enjoy!

Peach Crisp

Nutrition Info Per Serving: 41g Carbs, 5g Protein, 2g Fat, 212 Calories

No matter the season, it can be summer in your bowl! This dish is sweet, refreshing, and a great way to beat the heat (or sate your cravings). Add in its simplicity and you can't go wrong. In other words, it's a peach!

Peach Crisp

Makes:
5 Servings

Prep Time:
15 Minutes
Cook Time:
20 Minutes

Ingredients

- 5 large ripe peaches, sliced into bite size chunks
- 1 tbsp coconut sugar
- 1 tsp + 1 tsp cinnamon
- ⅔ cup oat flour
- ½ cup rolled oats
- ¼ tsp baking soda
- ¼ cup maple syrup
- ½ tsp vanilla extract
- Vanilla ice cream for serving, optional (see Yummy Basics)

Directions

1. Preheat your oven to 350 degrees F.
2. In a medium bowl, add the peach chunks, coconut sugar, and 1 tsp of cinnamon, and stir to coat the peaches.
3. Place the peaches on the bottom of a 9-inch square or circle glass baking pan.
4. In a small bowl, mix the rest of the ingredients until combined.
5. Take the oat mixture and evenly spread it out on top of the peaches.
6. Bake the peach crumble for 20 minutes. Serve hot with a scoop of vanilla ice cream if desired.

Apple Cinnamon Pudding

| 54 | **Nutrition Info Per Serving:** 61g Carbs, 3g Protein, 15g Fat, 398 Calories |

A super easy Canadian dessert that tastes just like apple pie! It takes much less time to make, and can be made by a baker with any skill level (beginner, lover, show-off, hobby cook, advanced), but is equally delicious and satisfying.

Ingredients

Crust
- 1 ½ cups all-purpose flour
- ½ cup vegan butter, at room temperature
- ⅓ cup cane sugar
- 2 tbsp apple sauce, unsweetened
- 1 tsp baking powder

Filling
- 3 apples, peeled and diced into small chunks
- 1 tbsp lemon juice
- 3 ¼ cups apple juice, unsweetened
- ¼ cup cane sugar
- 2 packets of vanilla pudding powder
  (or 80g corn starch and 1 tsp vanilla extract)
- 1 tbsp cinnamon

Directions

Apple Cinnamon Pudding

Makes:
8 Slices

Prep Time:
25 Minutes
Cook Time:
45 Minutes

1. Preheat the oven to 320 degrees F. Grease a 9-inch springform pan with some vegan butter and set aside.
2. In a medium bowl, add the flour, vegan butter, cane sugar, apple sauce, and baking powder. Use a pastry cutter or your hands to mix the ingredients together to form a dough. When the dough comes together, press it into the bottom of the pan and up the sides as well. Use a fork and press the dough against the sides of the pan.
3. Bake the crust for 10 minutes, then set aside.
4. Squirt the lemon juice onto the apples immediately after dicing them, so they don't go brown. Set aside.
5. In a medium pot, whisk together the apple juice, cane sugar, vanilla pudding powder, and cinnamon. Bring to a boil and cook until the mixture thickens up nicely – about 5 minutes. Add the apples and stir to combine.
6. Pour the filling into the crust and heat the oven to 350 degrees F. Bake the pudding for 35 minutes. Allow it to cool completely before serving.

Chapter 6

Ice Cream and Sorbets

Do you scream for ice cream? Do you say "yay" for sorbet? Then these recipes* are for you. Enjoy on a cone or in a bowl... preferably a large one.

*It's best to keep a couple of bananas in the freezer to make these recipes easier. For a basic ice cream recipe from scratch, please see Yummy Basics.

Mint Chocolate Chip Ice Cream

55	**Nutrition Info Per Serving:** 45g Carbs, 2g Protein, 17g Fat, 355 Calories

What two secrets are hidden behind this treat? First, the peppermint extract gives this dessert an incomparably creamy and refreshing taste. Second, Greens Powder from vegetables adds a minty green color to the ice cream, creating a truly genuine mint-dream-experience.

Mint Chocolate Chip Ice Cream

Makes:
4 Servings

Prep Time:
40 Minutes
Cook Time:
0 Minutes

Ingredients

- 1 14 oz can full fat coconut milk
- ⅔ cup cane sugar
- 1 ¼ tsp peppermint extract
- 1 tsp vanilla extract
- 1 tsp greens powder
  (such as barley grass, wheatgrass, spirulina, etc.)
- ⅓ cup mini chocolate chips

Directions

1. The day before, put your ice cream churning bowl into the freezer so it can freeze for at least 24 hours.
2. The next day, blend all of the ingredients, except for the chocolate chips, in a blender on high speed until well combined – for about 3 minutes.
3. Set up your ice cream maker and turn it on. Pour all of the contents from the blender into the ice cream maker. Add the chocolate chips into the mixture and allow it to churn until it resembles soft serve ice cream for 30 minutes.
4. You can eat the ice cream like this. If you prefer a more scoopable ice cream, transfer the mixture into a sturdy plastic container. Spread it out evenly and place a piece of plastic wrap right on top of the ice cream to prevent ice from forming on top. Put a lid on the container

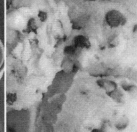

and freeze for at least 4-6 hours.
5. When ready to serve, scoop onto a cone or into a bowl and enjoy!

Mango Coconut Sorbet

| 56 | **Nutrition Info Per Serving:** 47g Carbs, 4g Protein, 8g Fat, 276 Calories |

Do you have five minutes to spare? Then grab your blender. This mango treat is perfect all year long (it's summer somewhere!). Sweet and healthy, have it over for dessert no matter the season, cause there's always a reason.

Raw, Gluten-Free, Low-Fat, Easy

Mango Coconut Sorbet

 Makes:
1 Serving

 Prep Time:
5 Minutes
Cook Time:
0 Minutes

Ingredients

- 1 ½ cups frozen ripe mango
- 2 tbsp water
- ¼ tsp vanilla extract
- 2 tbsp shredded coconut, unsweetened

Directions

1. In a blender or food processor, combine the mango, water, and vanilla until very smooth. If you need more water to get the blender going, add just a little bit at a time. You don't want to add too much and make the mixture too runny.
2. Scoop the sorbet into a bowl and top it with shredded coconut. Feel free to add additional toppings.

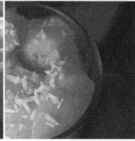

Strawberry Sorbet

| 57 | **Nutrition Info Per Serving:** 53g Carbs, 2g Protein, 1g Fat, 227 Calories |

Probably the tastiest sorbet in the world! This Strawberry Sorbet is the easiest frozen treat you will ever make. It takes just 4 minutes or less to prepare and you'll have a creamy, fruity, sweet sorbet that is naturally pure and healthy.

Strawberry Sorbet

 Makes:
1 Serving

 Prep Time:
4 Minutes
Cook Time:
0 Minutes

Ingredients

- 1 ½ cups frozen strawberries
- 3 tbsp maple syrup

Directions

1. Blend the ingredients in a high-powered blender or food processor until smooth. If you need to add a tiny bit of water to get the blender going, add just 1 teaspoon at a time.
2. Pour into a bowl and top with fresh strawberries if desired.

Ingredients

Oat-Raisin Cookies

Makes:
12 Cookies

Prep Time:
25 Minutes
Cook Time:
12 Minutes

- ¾ cup all-purpose flour
- ¾ cup rolled oats
- ¾ cup raisins
- ⅓ cup coconut sugar or brown sugar
- 1 tsp cinnamon
- ¾ tsp baking powder
- ¼ cup aquafaba
  (water from a can of chickpeas)
- 3 tbsp coconut oil, melted but not hot
- 2 tbsp almond butter
- 1 tsp vanilla extract

Directions

1. Preheat the oven to 350 degrees F. Line a baking tray with parchment paper and set aside.
2. In a large bowl, mix together the oats, flour, raisins, coconut sugar, cinnamon, and baking powder. Set aside.
3. In a separate bowl, whisk the aquafaba with either an electric mixer, or with a whisk by hand until soft peaks form.
4. Add the coconut oil, almond butter, and vanilla extract to the aquafaba and beat until incorporated.
5. Combine the wet and dry ingredients.
6. Form the batter into 12 small cookies. Line them onto the baking tray, bake for 12 minutes.

7. Allow the cookies to cool on a wire rack before consuming.

4-Ingredient Coconut Banana Cookies

66 | **Nutrition Info Per Serving:** 5g Carbs, 1g Protein, 7g Fat, 85 Calories

If you like bananas, then you'll go bananas for this dish: Health in cookie form – make them with your kids (you had them at "cookies")! It's very easy to make, only requires four ingredients, and is ready in three simple steps. Its versatility is a-"peeling": eat it for breakfast, dessert, or any time in between.

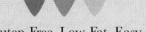

4-Ingredient Coconut Banana Cookies

 Makes:
12 Cookies

 Prep Time:
5 Minutes
Bake Time:
25 Minutes

Ingredients

- 2 ripe bananas
- 1 ½ cups packed shredded coconut, unsweetened
- 1 tsp cinnamon
- 1 tsp vanilla extract

Directions

1. Preheat your oven to 350 degrees F and line a baking sheet with parchment paper. Set aside.
2. In a food processor, pulse all of the ingredients until well combined.
3. Shape the dough into discs and place them on the baking sheet. Bake for 25 minutes, or until lightly golden.

Chocolate Peppermint Cookies

67 | **Nutrition Info Per Serving:** 11g Carbs, 3g Protein, 7g Fat, 121 Calories

These cookies will be waiting impatiently in your big biscuit glass to be nibbled on during the winter holidays. What is the secret that makes these cookies almost identical (if not better) to the original recipe? Aquafaba, which is the liquid that you find inside of a can of chickpeas! It works as an egg replacer and is perfect for vegan baking.

Dessert Idea for Christmas

Chocolate Peppermint Cookies

Makes:
20 Cookies

Prep Time:
15 Minutes
Cook Time:
11 Minutes

Ingredients

- ⅔ cup cocoa powder
- 1 cup coconut sugar
- 1 tsp baking soda
- Pinch of salt
- 1 cup natural almond butter
- ½ cup aquafaba
  (you will need 1-2 cans of chickpeas)
- 1 tsp vanilla extract
- ¾ tsp peppermint oil
- Powdered cane sugar for dusting

Directions

1. Preheat the oven to 350 degrees F and line 2 baking sheets with parchment paper. Set aside.
2. In a medium bowl, whisk together the cocoa powder, coconut sugar, baking soda, and salt. If the coconut sugar has some clumps, make sure to break them down as much as possible.
3. In a separate medium bowl, whisk together the rest of your ingredients.
4. Add the wet ingredients to the dry ingredients and mix with a spatula to combine.
5. Using your hands, scoop 1-2 tbsp of batter and form into small balls. Line them far apart on the tray because they spread very nicely.
6. Bake for 11 minutes. Allow the cookies to cool

on the tray before transferring them to a wire rack to cool completely.

7. Sift a few teaspoons of powdered sugar on top of each cookie. Enjoy!

Chocolate Bark

Nutrition Info Per Serving: 27g Carbs, 4g Protein, 18g Fat, 271 Calories

Do you need a gift idea? An ideal, homemade gift from the dessert kitchen is Chocolate Bark: a treat with a rustic look that's quick to prepare and still causes cries of ecstasy. You can switch out the toppings for virtually anything. The special thing that makes the big difference in this recipe: we used crystallized ginger for the sweet and spicy kick!

Gift Idea

160

Chocolate Bark

Makes:
4 Servings

Prep Time:
10 Minutes
Cook Time:
15 Minutes

Ingredients

- 1 cup dark chocolate
- 3 tbsp crystallized ginger, cut into small chunks
- 2 tbsp pumpkin seeds, roughly chopped

Directions

1. Line a small baking sheet or plate with parchment paper and set aside.
2. In a double boiler, melt the chocolate and whisk until smooth.
3. Pour the melted chocolate onto the parchment and spread around with a spatula until a nice thin, even layer of chocolate is achieved. It does not need to look perfect as chocolate bark is meant to look rustic.
4. Add the ginger and pumpkin seeds on top and spread evenly.
5. Place the pan in the fridge to allow the chocolate to fully harden – for about 15-20 minutes.
6. Break apart the chocolate into pieces, or use a knife to cut it. Enjoy!

Crispy Rice Treats

| 69 | **Nutrition Info Per Serving:** 22g Carbs, 0g Protein, 2g Fat, 108 Calories |

Crispy Rice Treats have Kathy reminiscing about childhood days. "I knew that every time I had one of those ooey gooey marshmallow squares in my lunch box at school that I would have a good day." You can find vegan marshmallows in the supermarket.

Crispy Rice Treats

Makes:
12 Servings

Prep Time:
10 Minutes
Cook Time:
0 Minutes

Ingredients

- 2 tbsp vegan butter
- 3 cups mini vegan marshmallows
- 1 tbsp non-dairy milk (e.g. almond milk)
- 1 tsp vanilla extract
- 2 ½ cups crispy rice cereal

Directions

1. In a large pot, melt the vegan butter. Add the marshmallows, milk, and vanilla, and stir until the marshmallows are melted.
2. Add the rice cereal and mix until evenly combined.
3. Press the mixture down into a pan that is approximately 6x10-inch and spread the mixture evenly.
4. Allow it to cool for about 20 minutes before cutting and serving.

Double Chocolate Chip Cookies

| 70 | **Nutrition Info Per Serving:** 25g Carbs, 2g Protein, 10g Fat, 205 Calories |

Most everybody loves chocolate chip cookies, and most everybody loves chocolate. What happens when you combine the two? Double chocolate chip cookies! What's not to love?!

Double Chocolate Chip Cookies

Makes:
24 Cookies

Prep Time:
20 Minutes
Cook Time:
15 Minutes

Ingredients

- 1 tbsp + 1 tsp ground flax
- ½ cup non-dairy milk, unsweetened (e.g. almond milk)
- 2 cups all-purpose flour
- ¾ cup cocoa powder
- 1 tsp baking soda
- Pinch of salt
- ¾ cup vegan butter, melted
- 1 ½ cups cane sugar
- 2 tsp vanilla extract
- ¾ cup vegan mini chocolate chips

Directions

1. Preheat the oven to 350 degrees F. Line 2 large baking sheets with parchment.
2. In a small bowl, whisk together the flax seeds and milk and set aside.
3. In a large bowl, add the flour, cocoa powder, baking soda, and salt, and whisk together until combined.
4. In a separate medium bowl, whisk together the vegan butter, sugar, and vanilla. Add the flax mixture and stir to combine.
5. Combine the wet and dry ingredients and mix well. Add the chocolate chips and stir until they are well distributed.
6. Form the dough into balls and flatten them with your hands to create a disk shape. Line them on the baking trays (there should be about 24) and bake for 15 minutes. Enjoy!

Chocolate Chip Granola Bars

71 | **Nutrition Info Per Serving:** 37g Carbs, 7g Protein, 16g Fat, 318 Calories

They taste a million times better than those from the store and you don't need an oven. Our no-bake granola bar recipe consists of wholesome ingredients such as dates, nuts, seeds, and oatmeal. The bars are prepared quickly – you'll be eating a delicious sweet treat in only a few minutes. A healthy dessert for any time of the day.

Chocolate Chip Granola Bars

Makes:
8 Granola Bars

Prep Time:
25 Minutes
Cook Time:
0 Minutes

Ingredients

- 1 cup soft dates, packed
- ¾ cup nuts/seeds
  (almonds, cashews, hazelnuts, walnuts, pecans, hemp seeds, or sunflower seeds, etc.)
- 1 ½ cups rolled oats
- ¼ cup maple syrup
- ¼ cup peanut butter
- 1 tsp vanilla extract
- ⅓ cup chocolate chips

Directions

1. Blend the dates in a food processor until they form a ball.
2. Add the dates into a bowl along with the nuts/seeds and oats. Mix until combined.
3. In a small pot, heat the maple syrup, peanut butter, and vanilla until warm.
4. Add this mixture to the date mixture along with the chocolate chips and stir everything until combined. Press the granola into an 8x8-inch square pan and freeze for 15 minutes.
5. Cut the granola into bars and store in the fridge.

Salted Caramel Chocolate Pretzel Bark

| 72 | **Nutrition Info Per Serving:** 32g Carbs, 4g Protein, 11g Fat, 243 Calories |

The delicious sweet-and-salty bite is not only visually an impressive dessert – it is also a sensational idea for the taste buds. Connoisseurs will be crazy about the unique triple combination of caramel, chocolate, and pretzels. P.S.: You can refer to the caramel sauce recipe from this book or use store-bought vegan caramel.

Salted Caramel Chocolate Pretzel Bark

Makes:
12 Servings

Prep Time:
25 Minutes
Cook Time:
0 Minutes

Ingredients

- 1 ½ cups dark chocolate
- 1 ½ cups salted pretzels
- ¼ cup caramel sauce
  (see Yummy Basics)

Directions

1. Use a double boiler to melt the chocolate.
2. While the chocolate is melting, line a small baking sheet with wax paper.
3. Reserve ¼ cup of the melted chocolate and set aside. Pour the remaining chocolate onto the wax paper and spread it out to create a thin rectangle that is about 15x20cm.
4. Take the pretzels and place them on top of the chocolate, placing each one side by side until all of the chocolate is covered. Use more or less pretzels if needed.
5. Pour the caramel sauce evenly on top.
6. Drizzle the remaining melted chocolate on top. Be creative and make crisscross lines, or swirls.
7. Place the tray into the freezer and freeze until set – about 10 minutes.
8. You can cut the pieces into squares with a knife, or you can break the pieces apart with your hands to create a more rustic look.
   Store in the freezer.

Apple Crumble Bars

73

Nutrition Info Per Serving: 37g Carbs, 4g Protein, 2g Fat, 192 Calories

Do you feel like a simple but healthy, low-fat dessert? Prepare these apple crumble pieces if you have apples left and impress your relatives with the juicy-crunchy treat! Or you can secretly make a batch and eat it all yourself... believe us, you won't be able to resist as soon as the delicious scent starts flowing out of the oven.

Dessert Idea for Thanksgiving

Ingredients

Crumble

- 1 ⅓ cups oat flour
- 1 cup large flake rolled oats
- ¼ tsp baking soda
- 1 ½ tsp cinnamon
- Pinch of salt
- ½ cup maple syrup
- ½ tsp vanilla extract

Apples

- 2 large apples
- 3 tbsp maple syrup
- 1 tbsp cinnamon
- ¼ tsp nutmeg
- ¼ tsp allspice
- ¼ tsp ginger powder

Directions

1. Preheat your oven to 350 degrees F and line an 8x8-inch baking tray with parchment paper.
2. In a large bowl, mix together the flour, oats, baking soda, cinnamon, salt, maple syrup, and vanilla until combined.
   Take ¾ of this mixture and press it into the bottom of the pan. Set aside.
3. Slice the apples very thinly with a knife or a mandolin. Add the apples to a large bowl and add the spices and maple syrup. Stir until the apples are well coated.
4. Layer the apples onto the base layer of the crumble. Take the remaining crumble and

Apple Crumble Bars

Makes:
9 Servings

Prep Time:
20 Minutes
Cook Time:
25 Minutes

sprinkle it on top of the apples.
5. Bake for 25 minutes and allow to cool completely before slicing. Enjoy!

Sugar Cookies

74

Nutrition Info Per Serving: 9g Carbs, 0g Protein, 2g Fat, 53 Calories

These coconut sugar cookies are a popular Christmas recipe in Scandinavia, and taste buttery and sweet. Sugar cookies are rolled and cut into shapes, or hand-shaped. They're the perfect cookie to make a huge batch of during the holidays, and they're so much fun to decorate!

Dessert Idea for Christmas

172

Ingredients

Dough
- ¾ cup powdered cane sugar
- ¼ cup + 2 tbsp coconut oil
- ¼ cup almond milk, unsweetened
- 1 tsp vanilla extract
- 1 ⅓ cups all-purpose flour
- ¼ tsp baking powder

Glaze
- ½ cup powdered cane sugar
- 1 ½ tsp water
- Greens powder, such as barley grass, wheatgrass, or spirulina, etc. (optional for green icing)

Sugar Cookies

Makes:
40-45 Cookies

Prep Time:
30 Minutes
Cook Time:
9-10 Minutes

Directions

1. Preheat the oven to 350 degrees F and line 2 large baking pans with parchment paper.
2. Gently heat the coconut oil and almond milk in a small saucepot until the coconut oil is melted, but the mixture is not hot.
3. Add this mixture along with the powdered sugar and vanilla into a stand mixer and mix on medium speed until combined for 3 minutes.
4. Add the flour and baking powder and mix until mostly combined. Dump the contents of the bowl onto a gently floured surface and knead into a dough.
5. Divide the dough in half and set one half aside. Roll out the other half into an even, thin layer about ¼ inch thick. Use cookie cutters to cut out pieces and lay them onto the parchment lined trays. Do the same with the other half of the dough. Gather any trimmings and roll the dough out again to cut out more cookies.
6. Bake the cookies for 9-10 minutes or until they are slightly golden brown. Allow the cookies to cool.
7. While the cookies are cooling, make your glaze. Whisk together the powdered sugar with the water. If the mixture is too thick, add a tiny bit of water at a time. If you want green icing, you can add a small spoon of powdered greens into the icing and whisk to combine. Add the desired amount until you achieve the color you like.
8. When the cookies are cooled, use a brush tool to brush the glaze onto the cookies. Allow to dry before serving.

Linzer Cookies

75 | **Nutrition Info Per Serving:** 10g Carbs, 1g Protein, 7g Fat, 108 Calories

It's only been a few days and the cookies are gone again – it's always that fast! Lovers of the famous Linzer Torte (see recipe in Chapter 4) will especially like the Linzer Cookie. The raspberry jam and ground almonds in the recipe complement each other perfectly.

Dessert Idea for Christmas

Ingredients

- ½ cup coconut oil, room temperature
- 2 tbsp cane sugar
- 1 tsp vanilla extract
- 1 ¼ cups all-purpose flour
- ½ cup ground almonds
- ¼ tsp baking soda
- Pinch of salt
- ⅓ cup raspberry jam
- ¼ cup powdered cane sugar

Linzer Cookies

Makes:
18-20 Cookies

Prep Time:
25 Minutes
Cook Time:
13-15 Minutes

Directions

1. Preheat the oven to 350 degrees F and line 2 baking trays with parchment paper.
2. In the bowl of a stand mixer, mix together the coconut oil, cane sugar, and vanilla for 2 min.
3. Add the flour, almonds, baking soda, and salt and mix until mostly combined.
4. Dump the dough onto a lightly floured work surface and use your hands to knead the dough into a ball.
5. Divide the dough in half and set one half aside. Roll out the other half into an even, thin layer about ¼ inch thick. Use a medium circular cookie cutter to cut out the cookies. Use a knife to spread a small amount of jam onto half of these cookies. For half of the cookies, use a very small circular cookie cutter and cut the center out of them, creating a "window". Add these pieces onto each cookie with jam to sandwich them. Do the same with the other half of the dough. Gather any trimmings and roll the dough out again. Lay cookies onto the parchment lined trays.
6. Bake the cookies for 13-15 minutes, or until they are slightly golden brown. Allow them to cool.
7. When the cookies are cooled, dust a small amount of powdered sugar onto each cookie. Serve and enjoy!

Chocolate Coconut Bars

76 **Nutrition Info Per Serving:** 21g Carbs, 3g Protein, 21g Fat, 293 Calories

Juicy coconut meets delicious chocolate: A little bit of South Sea magic fills the room with this treat. The bars are almost identical to the traditional chocolate bars with the familiar sweet coconut flake filling that we know from our childhood, and they are also so easy and quick to make. An impressive dessert for any candy bar lover!

Chocolate Coconut Bars

Makes:
10 Bars

Prep Time:
60 Minutes
Cook Time:
0 Minutes

Ingredients

- 1 ¾ cups shredded coconut, unsweetened
- The cream from a 14 oz can of full fat coconut milk
- 3 tbsp maple syrup
- 1 tsp vanilla extract
- 1 ½ cups dark chocolate

Directions

1. Using a blender or food processor, blend the first 4 ingredients until just combined – for less than one minute.
2. Line a baking tray with parchment. Form the coconut mixture into about 10 log shaped bars and line them on the tray.
   Freeze for 30 minutes.
3. When the bars are done, melt the chocolate in a double boiler. Dip each coconut log into the chocolate and fully coat it. Use a spoon to scoop the chocolate onto the bars if you want it to be less messy.
4. Allow the chocolate to harden before serving. Store in the fridge.

Chocolate Crackles

77 | **Nutrition Info Per Serving:** 6g Carbs, 0g Protein, 9g Fat, 110 Calories

Chocolate Crackles are a famous traditional Australian dessert that just happens to be vegan and gluten-free. This easily made treat is perfect for serving many people. They're individually wrapped and easy to transport to parties or events.

Gift Idea

Mini Chocolate Crackles

Makes:
35 Mini Crackles

Prep Time:
20 Minutes
Cook Time:
0 Minutes

Ingredients

- ½ cup coconut oil
- 2 cups crispy rice cereal
- ½ cup powdered cane sugar
- ½ cup shredded coconut, unsweetened
- 2 tbsp cocoa powder
- 1 tsp vanilla extract

Directions

1. Melt the coconut oil in a small pot until it is just melted. You don't want it to be hot. Set aside.
2. In a large bowl, add the rest of the ingredients and stir to combine. Add the coconut oil and mix until everything is evenly coated.
3. Lay out about 35 mini cupcake liners onto a baking sheet. Use a spoon to scoop the crackle mixture into each liner. Refrigerate for about 10-15 minutes, or until set. Store in the fridge until serving.

Banana Cinnamon Cookies

78 **Nutrition Info Per Serving:** 21g Carbs, 1g Protein, 5g Fat, 135 Calories

A cookie tin full of Banana Cinnamon Cookies should always be available –
not just at Christmas! As healthy treats, they're delicious the whole
year round. This recipe is delicious and easy, and will be fun to prepare with
your children.

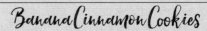

Banana Cinnamon Cookies

Makes:
16 Cookies

Prep Time:
20 Minutes
Cook Time:
10 Minutes

Ingredients

Dough

- ¾ cup cane sugar
- ⅓ cup coconut oil
- ¼ cup almond milk
- 1 ripe banana
- 1 tsp vanilla extract
- 1 ⅓ cups all-purpose flour
- 1 tsp cinnamon
- ½ tsp baking soda
- ¼ tsp baking powder

Cinnamon Sugar

- 3 tbsp cane sugar
- 1 tsp cinnamon

Directions

1. Preheat the oven to 375 degrees F and line a baking tray with parchment paper.
2. In the bowl of a stand mixer, mix together the sugar, coconut oil, almond milk, banana, and vanilla extract.
3. Add the flour, cinnamon, baking soda, and baking powder and mix until combined.
4. In a small bowl, mix together the cane sugar and cinnamon to make cinnamon sugar.
5. Form small balls from the dough and dip them in the cinnamon sugar to coat them completely. You should have 15-16 altogether.
6. Line them up on the baking tray, spread out evenly apart, and bake for 10 minutes. Cool completely before serving. Enjoy!

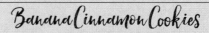

Banana Cinnamon Cookies

Makes:
16 Cookies

Prep Time:
20 Minutes
Cook Time:
10 Minutes

Ingredients

Dough
- ¾ cup cane sugar
- ⅓ cup coconut oil
- ¼ cup almond milk
- 1 ripe banana
- 1 tsp vanilla extract
- 1 ⅓ cups all-purpose flour
- 1 tsp cinnamon
- ½ tsp baking soda
- ¼ tsp baking powder

Cinnamon Sugar
- 3 tbsp cane sugar
- 1 tsp cinnamon

Directions

1. Preheat the oven to 375 degrees F and line a baking tray with parchment paper.
2. In the bowl of a stand mixer, mix together the sugar, coconut oil, almond milk, banana, and vanilla extract.
3. Add the flour, cinnamon, baking soda, and baking powder and mix until combined.
4. In a small bowl, mix together the cane sugar and cinnamon to make cinnamon sugar.
5. Form small balls from the dough and dip them in the cinnamon sugar to coat them completely. You should have 15-16 altogether.
6. Line them up on the baking tray, spread out evenly apart, and bake for 10 minutes. Cool completely before serving. Enjoy!

181

Ingredients

- 2 cups rolled oats
- 1 ¾ cups walnuts
- ¾ cup all-purpose flour
- ½ cup coconut sugar
- 1 tsp baking soda
- 1 tsp cinnamon
- Pinch of sea salt
- ½ cup maple syrup
- 3 tbsp coconut oil, melted
- 2 tbsp non-dairy milk, unsweetened (e.g. almond milk)
- 1 tsp vanilla extract
- ½ cup dates, chopped into small pieces
- ¼ cup chocolate chips

Directions

1. Preheat the oven to 350 degrees F and line 2 baking sheets with parchment paper.
2. In a food processor, blend together the oats and walnuts until they form a fine powder. Pour this mixture into a large bowl.
3. Add the flour, coconut sugar, baking soda, cinnamon, and salt, and stir to combine.
4. In a small bowl, whisk together the maple syrup, coconut oil, milk, and vanilla.
5. Add the wet ingredients to the dry ingredients and mix until combined. Add the chopped dates and chocolate chips and fold them into the batter.
6. Use your hands to form the cookies into disk shapes. Place them on the pans with enough room for them to grow.
7. Bake for 13 minutes in the middle rack of the oven. Remove from the oven and allow to cool completely before serving. Enjoy!

Chocolate Walnut Date Cookies

Makes:
20 Cookies

Prep Time:
20 Minutes
Cook Time:
13 Minutes

Chapter 8

Sweet Bites and Surprises

Quick and easy bites are a perfect option for anyone who doesn't want to eat an entire dessert – they just want a bite. These are ideal for holidays and other special occasions... like Tuesdays.

Red Velvet Fudge

80	**Nutrition Info Per Serving:** 10g Carbs, 2g Protein, 18g Fat, 211 Calories

This little delicacy with its soft-melting consistency, melts on your tongue... that must be the most sensational fudge you've ever tasted. It is gluten-free and refined-sugar-free. Where does the unbelievably bright color come from? The Red Velvet Fudge is naturally colored – with beet juice!

Red Velvet Fudge

 Makes:
16 Small Pieces of Fudge

 Prep Time:
10 Minutes
Cook Time:
At least 2 hours

Ingredients

- 1 cup coconut butter
- ¼ cup maple syrup
- ¼ cup beet juice
- 1 tbsp cocoa powder
- ½ tsp vanilla extract
- Pinch of salt

Directions

1. In a blender, blend together all of the ingredients until smooth.
2. Gently heat the mixture in a small saucepan and stir occasionally. Heat for at least 3 minutes or until the coconut butter starts to melt and the mixture looks shiny.
3. Pour the mixture into a 4x4 square pan lined with parchment (or a similar size pan). Allow the fudge to chill for at least 2 hours, or overnight.
4. When the fudge is fully set, cut into cubes and serve immediately, or store in the fridge until serving.

Chocolate Peppermint Cups

81 | **Nutrition Info Per Serving:** 24g Carbs, 6g Protein, 26g Fat, 348 Calories

Trick or Treat? This sweet treat is like a large version of a peppermint patty, but it's actually easier to make. The dessert captivates with its beautiful green color (guess where it comes from?), and goes great with Halloween.

Dessert Idea for a Gift/Halloween

Chocolate Peppermint Cups

Makes:
5 Chocolate Peppermint
Cups

Prep Time:
15 Minutes
Cook Time:
3-4 Hours

Ingredients

- 1 cup cashews
- ½ cup baby spinach
- ¼ cup maple syrup
- ¼ cup coconut oil
- ¼ cup almond milk
- 1 ¼ tsp peppermint oil
- ¼ cup chocolate chips, melted

Directions

1. In a high speed blender, blend all of the ingredients except for the chocolate. If you don't have a powerful blender, you'll need to soak the cashews for at least 3 hours. Blend until the mixture is smooth and fully combined.
2. Cut 5 large circular pieces of plastic wrap and insert them into the cavities of a muffin tin so that it is flat on the bottom and there is enough to cover the walls and to have an overhang.
3. Pour the mixture into the 5 cavities and distribute equally. Freeze for at least 3 hours, or until set.
4. When the cups are set, melt the chocolate over a double boiler.
5. Grab hold of the plastic wrap and lift each cup out of the muffin tin. Remove the plastic

wrap and drizzle the chocolate over the top of each cup. Be creative and make designs if you like. Serve immediately or place the cups on a plate lined with wax paper and return to the freezer until serving.

Chocolate Almond Filled Dates

82	**Nutrition Info Per Serving:** 26g Carbs, 2g Protein, 8g Fat, 180 Calories

Who doesn't love the trio of dates, chocolate, and almonds? This seriously simple yet impressive dessert is ideal for making a large batch of it (for a party or as a souvenir). It is very sweet and satisfies cravings in an instant.

Gift Idea

190

Chocolate Almond Filled Dates

Makes:
10 Dates

Prep Time:
15 Minutes
Cook Time:
0 Minutes

Ingredients

- 10 Medjool dates
- About 15 almonds
- ¾ cup dark chocolate
- 10 almonds,
  roughly chopped into small pieces

Directions

1. Take each date, create a slit to open them up, and remove all of the pits.
2. Stuff each date with 1 or 2 almonds, whatever fits nicely inside, and close the dates back up again.
3. Melt the chocolate in a double boiler. Coat each date with chocolate, then place them on a plate lined with wax paper and allow the chocolate to harden.
4. Dip each date again to coat it a second time and line them on the parchment again. Sprinkle the crushed almonds on top and allow the chocolate to harden. Chill, serve, and enjoy!

1-Ingredient Peanut Butter Cups

83 | **Nutrition Info Per Serving:** 10g Carbs, 3g Protein, 10g Fat, 135 Calories

Peanut butter cups are a favorite of just about everyone who's conscious. Channel Halloween any time of year with these delicious treats. They can't get much easier: 2 ingredients and 6 steps. They're sure to be a hit among all the boys and ghouls!

Dessert Idea for Halloween

192

2-Ingredient Peanut Butter Cups

 Makes:
15 Peanut Butter Cups

 Prep Time:
30 Minutes
Cook Time:
0 Minutes

Ingredients

- 1 cup dark chocolate
- ½ cup natural smooth peanut butter

Directions

1. Place 15 mini muffin liners on a plate or tray and set aside.
2. Melt ½ cup of the chocolate in a double boiler. You don't want to melt all of the chocolate at this time, because it will begin to firm up. Distribute the melted chocolate between the 15 liners. To do this, scoop around 1 tsp of chocolate with a small spoon into each liner and spread evenly on the bottom of the liners, and around the sides to create a base for the cups.
3. Refrigerate for around 5 minutes, or until the chocolate is set.
4. Scoop the peanut butter into the cups and distribute evenly.
5. Melt the other ½ cup of dark chocolate in a double boiler and top off all of the cups with the chocolate.
6. Place in the fridge again until the chocolate is set. Serve and store leftovers in the fridge.

Simple Chocolate Sea Salt Fudge

84 | **Nutrition Info Per Serving:** 12g Carbs, 2g Protein, 12g Fat, 180 Calories

Do you need a fast treat for a party? This fudge will budge to your schedule; you can make it in minutes! This fudge is a sweet, decadent little treat. Just pop it in the fridge and it'll be ready to serve by dessert time!

Simple Chocolate Sea Salt Fudge

Makes:
About 30 Fudge Pieces

Prep Time:
5 Minutes
Cook Time:
0 Minutes

Ingredients

- 1 cup full fat coconut milk
- 1 tsp vanilla extract
- ¾ cup powdered cane sugar
- 3 cups dark chocolate (minimum of 80%)
- Sea salt

Directions

1. Line an 8x8-inch square pan with parchment paper. Set aside.
2. In a small saucepan, gently heat coconut milk and vanilla extract. Do not let it boil, just gently simmer.
3. When the milk begins to gently steam, sift in the powdered sugar and whisk until smooth. Take the pot off the heat.
4. Add the chocolate and whisk until it is melted and fully combined.
5. Pour the fudge into your pan and distribute evenly.
6. If your pan is hot, allow it to cool before putting it in the fridge. Refrigerate for about 2 hours, or until the fudge is firm.
7. Sprinkle some sea salt on top of the fudge. Cut into squares and serve. Store in the fridge.

Peanut Butter Balls

85   **Nutrition Info Per Serving:** 8g Carbs, 1g Protein, 2g Fat, 48 Calories

Peanut Butter Balls are reminiscent of Kathy's childhood because her family always had them on the dessert table every Easter. The fun combination of peanut butter, maple syrup, and cereal makes this bite-sized dessert irresistible – especially for kids. Watch the balls before your eyes...

Dessert Idea for Easter

196

Peanut Butter Balls

 Makes:
16-18 Balls

 Prep Time:
20 Minutes
Cook Time:
0 Minutes

Ingredients

- ½ cup natural peanut butter
- ½ cup maple syrup
- ¼ cup powdered cane sugar
- ½ tsp vanilla extract
- 2 cups crispy rice cereal

Directions

1. In a small pot, gently heat all of the ingredients together except for the cereal. Whisk it until smooth, and heat until it is warm, not hot.
2. Pour the rice cereal into a medium bowl. Add the peanut butter mixture and mix everything until is evenly combined. Allow this to cool for 5 minutes.
3. Line a small baking tray with parchment paper. Wet your hands with water and form small balls. Line them up on the tray side by side. If your hands begin to get sticky, wash them and wet them again. You may need to do this 2-3 times.
4. Place the balls in the freezer for about 10 minutes and serve immediately. If you plan to serve them later, you can just put them in the fridge and store them there.

Chocolate Orange Truffles

86	**Nutrition Info Per Serving:** 14g Carbs, 2g Protein, 1g Fat, 73 Calories

Christmas is hard to imagine without these heavenly chocolate truffles. They are also suitable for New Years or as a special gift. Do you know which secret ingredient is in our recipe? Black beans! But we guarantee nobody will ever taste them.

Dessert Idea for Christmas/New Year

Gluten-Free, Low-Fat, Easy

Chocolate Orange Truffles

Makes:
12 Truffles

Prep Time:
15 Minutes

Cook Time:
0 Minutes

Ingredients

- ¾ cup soft dates, chopped into pieces
- ¾ cup black beans
- ¾ cup cocoa powder
- ¼ cup maple syrup
- 3 tbsp orange juice
- Orange zest from 1 medium orange
- 1 tbsp cocoa powder

Directions

1. Blend all of the ingredients except for 1 tbsp of cocoa powder, in a food processor until smooth and combined – about 2-3 minutes.
2. Roll the dough into about 12 balls.
   Add 1 tbsp of cocoa powder into a small bowl and place each truffle in the bowl 1 at a time, to coat them.
3. Refrigerate then serve.

Sweet Potato Chips

87 | **Nutrition Info Per Serving:** 31g Carbs, 4g Protein, 7g Fat, 223 Calories

We're giddy with excitement... Baked sweet potato chips are a crispy sweet-savory snack – and impossible to stop eating! All you need are 3 ingredients. They're so easy to make, they're much healthier, and so full of flavor – you'll never know the difference.

Sweet Potato Chips

Makes:
2 Servings

Prep Time:
10 Minutes
Cook Time:
20-25 Minutes

Ingredients

- 2 medium sweet potatoes, sliced into thin pieces
- 1 tbsp coconut oil
- ½ tsp salt

Directions

1. Preheat the oven to 400 degrees F and line 2 baking trays with parchment paper.
2. Slice the sweet potatoes into thin slices with a mandolin or a sharp knife. The mandolin is very beneficial to use since you can cut them very thinly and the chips will all be the same thickness, which will be easier for cooking and will prevent burning.
3. Add the sliced sweet potatoes into a large bowl, along with the oil and salt and use your hands to mix them and coat the potatoes evenly.
4. Place the sweet potatoes on the baking trays in a single layer. Bake for 20-25 minutes, until crispy.
5. Allow them to cool completely before serving. Store in an airtight container.

Almond Butter & Jam Surprise

88 | **Nutrition Info Per Serving:** 23g Carbs, 5g Protein, 15g Fat, 253 Calories

Sweet and salty – crunchy and gooey. This is like the adult version of a nut butter and jam sandwich, turned into dessert. It won't only be the kids who thank you for it.

Ingredients

Crust
- 1 cup rolled oats
- 1 cup almonds
- 2 tbsp coconut sugar
- Pinch of salt
- ¼ cup coconut oil, melted

Topping
- 1 cup frozen or fresh strawberries
- ½ cup strawberry jam
- 5 tsp almond butter

Directions

1. Preheat the oven to 350 degrees F, line an 8x8-inch square baking pan with parchment paper.
2. In a food processor, blend the oats, almonds, coconut sugar, and salt until it is fine. Add the melted coconut oil and blend again until everything is combined.
3. Press the mixture down into the bottom of the pan and spread it out evenly.
4. Bake the crust for 15 minutes near the bottom rack of your oven.
5. While the crust is baking, heat the strawberries and the jam in a saucepan for about 5 minutes.
6. Remove the crust from the oven but keep the oven on and at the same temperature. Pour the jam mixture onto the crust and spread it out evenly.
7. Dollop 1 tsp of almond butter into each corner of the pan and also in the center. Use the end

Almond Butter & Jam Surprise

Makes:
9 Bars

Prep Time:
15 Minutes
Cook Time:
28 Minutes

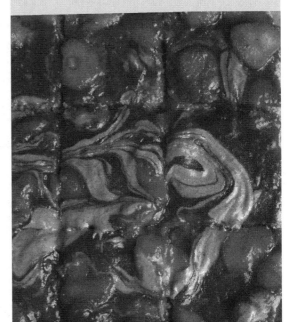

of a spoon to swirl the almond butter into the jam.

8. Return the pan to the oven for another 13 minutes. Remove from the oven and allow it to cool completely before slicing. Enjoy!

Chapter 9

Drink me Darlings

Sometimes dessert comes in a glass. Gulp down these darling options and give your sweet tooth bragging rights. They're perfect on a hot summer day (but also hard to resist on a cold winter's night).

Pineapple Float

Nutrition Info Per Serving: 57g Carbs, 2g Protein, 16g Fat, 385 Calories

Sweet-Sour, Sun, Fun! A pineapple float that is so refreshing you'll feel like you're in the tropics, no matter where you are. This recipe will transport you to paradise.

Pineapple Float

Makes:
1 Serving

Prep Time:
20 Minutes
Cook Time:
0 Minutes

Ingredients

- 1 ½ cups frozen pineapple
- ¾ cup water
- 1 tbsp maple syrup, or to taste
- 1 large scoop vegan vanilla ice cream (see Yummy Basics in this book)

Directions

1. Take the pineapple out of the freezer and allow it to thaw for 15 minutes.
2. Blend all of the ingredients except for the ice cream in a blender until smooth.
3. Scoop 1 generous portion of your favorite vegan vanilla ice cream on top. Drink with a straw or eat with a spoon.

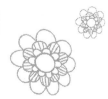

Banana Milkshake

| 90 | **Nutrition Info Per Serving:** 54g Carbs, 3g Protein, 33g Fat, 530 Calories |

We're throwing it back a few decades with this popular classic of creamy shakes: Banana Milkshake... with vegetable milk! For this recipe you can use your favorite store bought vegan vanilla ice cream or make your own (see Yummy Basics), mix it with banana and... enjoy, enjoy, enjoy.

Banana Milkshake

Makes:
1 Serving

Prep Time:
5 Minutes
Cook Time:
0 Minutes

Ingredients

- 3 scoops vegan vanilla ice cream
  (Recipe see Yummy Basics)
- 1 banana, ripe
- Splash of non-dairy milk,
  unsweetened
  (e.g. soymilk, oat milk, almond milk)

Directions

1. Blend all ingredients in a blender
   until smooth.
2. Serve in a tall glass with a straw and enjoy!

Sweet Tooth Milkshake

91 | **Nutrition Info Per Serving:** 71g Carbs, 20g Protein, 43g Fat, 743 Calories

The ideal refreshment for magical summer days or long summer nights. In just 5 minutes you'll be sipping on this decadent from-scratch milkshake. But beware! Our sweet tooth milkshake with peanut butter and chocolate chips is addictive.

Sweet Tooth Milkshake

Makes:
1 Milkshake

Prep Time:
5 Minutes

Cook Time:
0 Minutes

Ingredients

- 2 bananas, frozen
- ½ cup non-dairy milk, unsweetened (e.g. almond milk)
- ¼ cup all natural peanut butter
- 1 tbsp chocolate chips
- ¼ tsp vanilla extract
- ¼ tsp cinnamon
- Additional chocolate chips, cinnamon, and chopped peanuts for garnish

Directions

1. In a blender, blend all of the ingredients, except for the garnish, until smooth.
2. Pour the milkshake into a tall glass and garnish with chocolate chips, chopped peanuts, and a dash of cinnamon. Serve immediately.

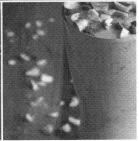

Iced Mocha Latte

| 92 | **Nutrition Info Per Serving:** 41g Carbs, 1g Protein, 1g Fat, 176 Calories |

If you like to drink espresso, mocha, or coffee, this is the place for you. With this twist on a classic ice cream coffee, you can be your own barista at home. Make your own fancy coffee beverage (for a fraction of the price) and enjoy it on hot days.

Iced Mocha Latte

Makes:
1 Serving

Prep Time:
30 Minutes
Cook Time:
0 Minutes

Ingredients

- ½ cup brewed coffee
- ¼ cup non-dairy milk, unsweetened (e.g. almond milk)
- 3 tbsp maple syrup
- 2 tsp cocoa powder, unsweetened
- ¼ tsp vanilla extract
- 6 ice cubes

Directions

1. Brew your coffee according to package directions and allow it to cool in a cold place for at least 30 minutes. Place it in the freezer if possible to cool it down quickly.
2. When the coffee is cooled, add all of the ingredients to a blender except for the ice. Blend all of the ingredients until combined.
3. Add the ice cubes and pulse until the ice is crushed into small chunks. Serve and enjoy!

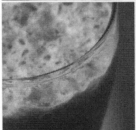

Chapter 10

Yummy Basics

Anyone who loves dessert knows that the magic is often in the sauce. These recipes provide delicious vegan options. Your taste buds and your body will thank you.

Chocolate Hazelnut Spread

93 | **Nutrition Info Per Serving:** 12g Carbs, 6g Protein, 26g Fat, 299 Calories

First we could not trust our taste buds... then... we were completely thrilled! This Chocolate Hazelnut Spread tastes just like the world famous nut nougat spread that is 100% addictive. So many of us (all of us) think this recipe is even better than the original! Roasted hazelnuts make this cream nutritious and very, very delicious.

 Makes:
8 Servings

 Prep Time:
35 Minutes
Cook Time:
15 Minutes

Ingredients

- 2 cups hazelnuts
- ½ cup dark chocolate
- 1 tbsp maple syrup, room temperature
- ½ tsp vanilla extract
- Pinch of salt

Directions

1. Pour the hazelnuts on a baking tray in a single layer and bake for 15 minutes at 350 degrees F. You can also buy hazelnuts that are already roasted and skip this step.
2. When the nuts are done roasting, pour them onto a clean tea towel or large sheet of paper towel. Use another tea towel or paper towel and rub the hazelnuts to get the skins off. This can take some time, but do your best, as the spread tastes best with minimal skins.
3. Add the clean hazelnuts into a high-powered blender that is suitable for nut butters and blend until smooth and creamy.
4. Using a double boiler, melt the dark chocolate until fully melted. Add the chocolate, maple syrup, vanilla, and salt into the blender and blend until fully incorporated.
5. Store in an airtight container in the fridge. It will harden in the fridge a bit but will melt again on warm toast. Enjoy!

217

Chocolate Sauce

94 **Nutrition Info Per Batch:** 60g Carbs, 6g Protein, 20g Fat, 437 Calories

This is an all-purpose chocolate sauce that can be paired with many desserts. The bonus is that it is made with simple ingredients and without added oils or refined sugar.

Chocolate Sauce

Makes:
About 1 Cup

Prep Time:
5 Minutes
Cook Time:
0 Minutes

Ingredients

- ½ cup full fat coconut milk
- ¼ cup cocoa powder
- ¼ cup maple syrup
- ¼ tsp vanilla extract

Directions

1. In a small pot, combine all of the ingredients and bring to a gentle boil. Whisk everything together, so that it is smooth and the cocoa powder is well incorporated.
2. Pour immediately on your dessert. You can store this in the fridge for future use. The sauce will thicken up when refrigerated, so you will want to heat it up again before using.

Easy Caramel Sauce

95	**Nutrition Info Per Serving:** 39g Carbs, 1g Protein, 15g Fat, 298 Calories

This caramel sauce is easy to make from just four ingredients, and has a natural sweetness. It tastes like the real thing! Serve this with apple or banana slices... or top virtually any dessert (pancakes, waffles, or ice cream, etc.) with this delicious sauce.

Easy Caramel Sauce

Makes:
1 Cup Caramel Sauce

Prep Time:
30 Minutes
Cool Time:
2+ Hours

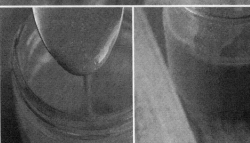

Ingredients

- 1 400ml can full fat coconut milk (not "light")
- ¾ cup coconut sugar
- Pinch of salt
- 1 tsp vanilla extract

Directions

1. In a small saucepan, whisk together coconut milk, sugar, and salt. Do not add the vanilla extract yet.
2. Heat this mixture over high heat until it comes to a boil. Once it is boiling, reduce the heat to low and bring the mixture to a gentle simmer for 25-30 minutes. It will thicken up slightly.
3. Remove the pot from the heat and whisk in the vanilla extract. Allow it to cool on your counter enough before placing it in the fridge.
4. Place the pot in the fridge until it is completely cooled and becomes thicker. If you need to speed this process up, you can put it in the freezer, stirring occasionally so it does not freeze.
5. Serve with any dessert you desire, or use it as a dip.

Classic Pie Crust

96   **Nutrition Info Per Batch:** 113g Carbs, 15g Protein, 55g Fat, 1040 Calories

Traditional pie crust is typically filled with lard or vegetable shortening which is very processed and bad for your health. This pie crust tastes flaky and tender just like a traditional pie crust.

Easy

Classic Pie Crust

Makes:
1 9-inch Pie Crust

Prep Time:
10 Minutes
Cook Time:
0 Minutes

Ingredients

- 1 cup + 2 tbsp all-purpose flour
- 2 ½ tsp cane sugar
- Pinch of salt
- ¼ cup coconut oil
- ¼ cup cold water

Directions

1. In a large bowl, sift and combine flour, cane sugar, and salt.
2. Add the coconut oil and combine with your hands until it is crumbly but no oil clumps remain.
3. Add the cold water into the dough and combine until a sticky dough forms. Add additional water if needed, 1 tbsp at a time.
4. Flour your work surface and a rolling pin. Roll the dough onto the surface and roll it out into a disk shape, large enough to fit your pie pan.
5. Place the dough in your pie pan and spread it out evenly, cutting off any excess trim. Add your filling and bake according to your pie recipe.

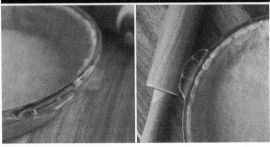

223

Vanilla Pastry Cream

| 97 | **Nutrition Info Per Batch:** 88g Carbs, 14g Protein, 50g Fat, 865 Calories |

How to make a sweet cream filling that completes your pastry perfectly: This sweet and luscious vanilla pastry cream can be used for a variety of desserts such as in a swiss roll cake, eclairs, cream puffs, napoleons, tarts, cakes, and many other pastries.

Vanilla Pastry Cream

Makes:
About 2 Cups of Cream

Prep Time:
5 Minutes
Cook Time:
0 Minutes

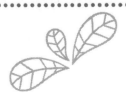

Ingredients

- ½ cup cashews (soaked overnight)
- ¼ cup + 1 tbsp maple syrup
- ¼ cup coconut oil, melted
- 1 tsp vanilla extract
- The cream from 1 15 oz can full fat coconut milk (chilled in the fridge overnight)

Directions

1. Blend the cashews, maple syrup, coconut oil, and vanilla extract in a blender until smooth.
2. Open up the can of coconut milk. Scoop out the thick cream and discard the water (or you can use it for smoothies or in other recipes). Add the cream to the blender and blend again until smooth.
3. Pour the cream into a container and allow to chill for at least 1 hour before using.

Almond Milk

Nutrition Info Per Serving: 4g Carbs, 2g Protein, 3g Fat, 40 Calories

Making almond milk is so easy and will save you money too! Some store bought almond milks have fillers, binders, and sweeteners that aren't necessary. It can be used for cooking and baking. If you want to enjoy the milk unsweetened, or use for one of the recipes in this book, just skip the dates and the vanilla extract.

Almond Milk

Makes:
2 Glasses
Prep Time:
10 Minutes
Cook Time:
0 Minutes

Ingredients

- 1 cup almonds
- 2 cups water
- 2 soft dates such as Medjool
- ½ tsp vanilla extract

Directions

1. Soak your almonds in a container with enough water to cover the almonds, for at least 12 hours.
2. When the almonds are finished soaking, drain and rinse them. Add them to a high-powered blender with the rest of the ingredients and blend on high until combined.
3. Strain the milk into a large bowl through a nut milk bag. You can save the pulp for other recipes or discard it. Store the milk in a jar or pitcher in the fridge until serving.

Oat Milk

| 99 | **Nutrition Info Per Serving:** 25g Carbs, 4g Protein, 2g Fat, 147 Calories |

Oat milk is the perfect milk to make at home if you want a plant milk that is easy to make and nut free. It's very creamy and has a natural hint of sweetness. Perfect for granola, smoothies, coffee, and more! If you want to enjoy the milk unsweetened, or use for one of the recipes in this book, just skip the dates and the vanilla extract.

Favorite Desserts Made VEGAN!

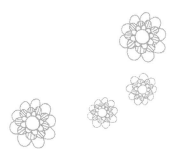

Oat Milk

Makes:
3 Glasses

Prep Time:
10 Minutes
Cook Time:
0 Minutes

Ingredients

- 3 cups water
- 1 cup rolled oats
- 4-6 dates (4 large or 6 small)
- 1 tsp vanilla extract

Directions

1. Blend all of the ingredients in a blender until combined and smooth.
2. Pour the milk through a nut milk bag and strain the oat pulp. If you like a thick and creamy milk, you can skip the straining.
3. Store in the fridge until serving.

Coconut Whipped Cream

100	Nutrition Info Per Batch: 19g Carbs, 1g Protein, 4.5g Fat, 130 Calories

Coconut Whipped Cream is one of those desserts that tastes exactly like conventional whipped cream and it's made of three simple ingredients.
Tip: Keep a few cans of coconut milk in the fridge at all times so you don't have to wait for your cream to refrigerate.

Raw, Gluten-Free, Easy

Coconut Whipped Cream

Makes:
About 1 ½ Cups

Prep Time:
24 Hours
Cook Time:
0 Minutes

Ingredients

- 1 x 15 oz can full fat coconut milk
- 1 tbsp + 1 tsp maple syrup
- 1 ½ tsp vanilla extract

Directions

1. Refrigerate your can of coconut milk for a minimum of 24 hours. Do not skip this step as it is absolutely critical. If you already have coconut milk in the fridge, you can skip this step.
2. Remove the coconut milk from the fridge and flip over the can. Open up the can and you should have coconut water on top and thick coconut cream underneath. Pour out the coconut water and store it in your fridge for another recipe. You can use it in smoothies and other desserts.
3. Remove all of the coconut cream in the can and place it in the bowl of stand mixer. Add the maple syrup and vanilla and whip on medium/high speed for at least 10 minutes, or until the cream is nice and fluffy and completely smooth.
4. Chill in the fridge until using. It will firm up in the fridge and soften again at room temperature. If you want you can whip it again just before using. Serve with fresh fruit, pies, cakes, or any dessert!

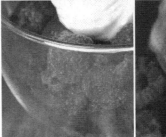

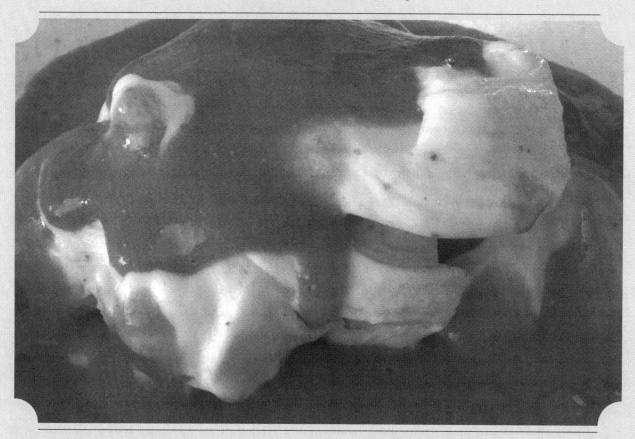

Nicecream
Vanilla Ice Cream

101	**Nutrition Info Per Serving:** 75g Carbs, 2g Protein, 0g Fat, 230 Calories

Ice cream, but nice. The healthiest ice cream in the world. No wonder that it's called Nicecream but it's also known as Nanacream (from Banana Cream). Perfect if you have children who don't like eating fruit – they will love this ice cream! Serve with a pureed strawberry sauce or with finely pureed mango.

A recipe for a chocolate ice cream can be found in Chapter 6: Ice Cream and Sorbets.

Vanilla Ice Cream (Nicecream)

Makes:
2 Servings

Prep Time:
3 Hours freezing time+
5 Minutes preparation
Cook Time:
0 Minutes

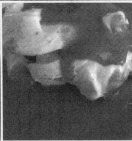

Ingredients

- 4 large frozen bananas
- 1 tsp vanilla extract (if required)

Directions

1. Cut the bananas into slices on a plate and place them in a freezer for 3 hours. If you already have frozen bananas, let them defrost for about 15-20 minutes before blending, but with freshly frozen bananas the result will taste even better.
2. Blend the bananas and the vanilla extract together in a high-powered blender or food processor until smooth. Decorate with pureed sauce and favorite fruit. Serve immediately and enjoy!

Vanilla Frosting

102 | **Nutrition Info Per Batch:** 360g Carbs, 0g Protein, 108g Fat, 2385 Calories

A quick and easy all-purpose vanilla frosting that can be used for a variety of desserts. This recipe makes about 2 cups of frosting and covers a 9-inch cake. You can easily double these measurements if you have a large cake.

Vanilla Frosting

Makes:
About 2 cups of frosting

Prep Time:
10 Minutes
Cook Time:
0 Minutes

Ingredients

- 3 ¾ cups powdered cane sugar
- ¼ cup non-dairy milk, unsweetened (e.g. almond milk)
- 3 tbsp vegan butter
- 1 tsp vanilla extract

Directions

1. In a stand mixer, mix all of the ingredients together until smooth and fluffy – at least 5 minutes or more.
2. Ice your dessert immediately.

Chocolate Frosting

| 103 | **Nutrition Info Per Serving:** 216g Carbs, 21g Protein, 182g Fat, 2575 Calories |

This frosting is to die for! An all-purpose chocolate frosting that is super easy to make. It will have you licking every last drop out of the bowl.

Chocolate Frosting

Makes:
About 2 cups

Prep Time:
10 Minutes
Chill Time:
20-40 Minutes

Ingredients

- 1 ½ cups chocolate chips
- ⅓ cup + 2 tbsp powdered cane sugar
- ¼ cup + 2 tbsp non-dairy milk, unsweetened (e.g. almond milk)
- ¼ cup + 2 tbsp coconut oil
- 1 ½ tsp vanilla extract

Directions

1. Add all of the frosting ingredients into a medium saucepan and melt on medium heat. Whisk until all of the chocolate is melted and the ingredients are fully combined.
2. Pour the frosting into the bowl of your stand mixer. Place the stand mixer in the freezer to allow it to firm up. Depending on how cold your freezer is, this can take anywhere from 2045 minutes. Keep an eye on it because you don't want it to get too firm.
3. When the frosting is cool enough, place the bowl in the stand mixer and whip the frosting. Beat it on medium/high for about 2 minutes. Don't overbeat it because the frosting will begin to firm up and will be difficult to spread. Ice your dessert immediately.

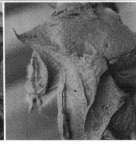

A Few Things Worth Noting...

A quick "egg-ucation"

There are several different ingredients you can use as a substitute for eggs, including ingredients already in your pantry. You can make flax or chia eggs by combining ground flax or chia with water. If your dish needs more moisture or you would like to limit fat, mashed bananas or apple sauce make excellent alternatives.

A small conversion table:

- 1 tablespoon of chia seeds soaked in 3 tablespoons of water replaces 1 egg
- 1 teaspoon of flaxseed mixed with 4 tsp of water replaces 1 egg
- ½ a crushed banana replaces 1 egg
- 3 tablespoons of apple sauce replaces 1 egg

Tip 1: Take your time. Play with the different ingredients and their quantities. Assess which alternate product works best and gives you the result you want.

Tip 2: Read the next information about Aquafaba – another amazing egg alternative.

The (non) milky way

Many non-dairy milks contain a lot of sugar, oils, flavorings, and supplements. Simple, pure, unsweetened plant milk most closely resembles dairy milk. All of the recipes suggest using unsweetened plant milk so that it doesn't affect the flavor of the recipes. Almond milk and soy milk work well in most recipes.

Tip: Did you know plant milk is easy and inexpensive to make? In the Yummy Basics section you will find a recipe for homemade almond milk. If you do not tolerate nuts or want to use a second tasty milk for your desserts, you can make milk from oatmeal.

Aquafaba?
It's aqua-fabulous!

Aquafaba, literally bean water, is the cooking fluid or soaking water of chickpeas (beans and other legumes). It can take over the functions of an emulsifier, raising agent, and foaming agent, and act as a substitute for egg whites. Pleasantly tasteless, it gives dishes the desired texture.

Apropos: The wet nutmeg remaining in the production of almond milk can also be used as cheese or dried (and used as flour).

Oils and Fats?
Pure plant-based variants

Margarine is often used as a butter substitute in vegan dishes. However, many margarines contain unhealthy hydrogenated and refined fats. Earth Balance is a better substitute because it contains smaller amounts. Coconut fat / oil is also an alternative for vegan cuisine.

Measurement Conversions

Liquid/Volume Measurements (approximate)

1 teaspoon = 1/6 fluid ounce (oz.) = 1/3 tablespoon = 5 ml
1 tablespoon = 1/2 fluid ounce (oz.) = 3 teaspoons = 15 ml
1 fluid ounce (oz.) = 2 tablespoons = 1/8 cup = 30 ml
1/4 cup = 2 fluid ounces (oz.) = 4 tablespoons = 60 ml
1/3 cup = 2 2/3 fluid ounces (oz.) = 5 1/3 tablespoons = 80 ml
1/2 cup = 4 fluid ounces (oz.) = 8 tablespoons = 120 ml
2/3 cup = 5 1/3 fluid ounces (oz.) = 1o 2/3 tablespoons = 160 ml
3/4 cup = 6 fluid ounces (oz.) = 12 tablespoons = 180 ml
7/8 cup = 7 fluid ounces (oz.) = 14 tablespoons = 210 ml
1 cup = 8 fluid ounces (oz.) = 1/2 pint = 240 ml
1 pint = 16 fluid ounces (oz.) = 2 cups = 1/2 quart = 475 ml
1 quart = 4 cups = 32 fluid ounces (oz.) = 2 pints = 950 ml
1 liter = 1.055 quarts = 4.22 cups = 2.11 pints = 1000 ml
1 gallon = 4 quarts = 8 pints = 3.8 liters

Dry/Weight Measurements (approximate)

1 ounce (oz.) = 30 grams (g)
2 ounces (oz.) = 55 grams (g)
3 ounces (oz.) = 85 grams (g)
1/4 Pound (lb.) = 4 ounces (oz.) = 125 grams (g)
1/2 pound (lb.) = 8 ounces (oz.) = 240 grams (g)
3/4 pound (lb.) = 12 ounces (oz.) = 375 grams (g)
1 pound (lb.) = 16 ounces (oz.) = 455 grams (g)
2 pounds (lbs.) = 32 ounces (oz.) = 910 grams (g)
1 kilogram (kg) = 2.2 pounds (lbs.) = 1000 gram (g)

Favorite Desserts made VEGAN!

Disclaimer & Legal

Mention of specific companies, organizations or authorities in this book does not imply endorsement by the publisher, nor does mention of specific companies, organizations, or authorities imply that they endorse the book. Further, the publisher does not have any control over and does not assume any responsibility for author or third-party websites or their content.

Every effort has been made to ensure the accuracy of the information presented und any claims made. However it is the responsibility of the reader to ensure the suitability of the product and recipe for their particular needs. If you or anyone likely to be consuming food from the *Favorite Desserts ma•e VEGAN!*, has any food allergies or sensitivities, it is your responsibility to ensure all ingredients are checked before use. The author und publisher make no guarantee as to the availability of products in this book. Many ingredients vary in size und texture und these differences may affect the outcome of some recipes. In no way is the *Favorite Desserts ma•e VEGAN!* and those attached to it, intended to replace, countermund, or conflict with the advice given to you by your own doctor or other physician. If you know or suspect that you have a health problem, professional medical or nutritional advice should be sought for any specific issues before embarking on any dietary changes. The ultimate decision concerning care should be made between you und your doctor. We strongly recommend that you follow their advice. Information in the *Favorite Desserts ma•e VEGAN!* cookbook is general and is offerote with no guarantees on the part of the author or the publisher. The author und publisher disclaim all liability in connection with the use of the *Favorite Desserts ma•e VEGAN!*. Neither the publisher nor the author disengaged in rendering professional advice or services to the individual reader. Neither the author nor the publisher shall be liable or responsible for any loss or damage allegedly arising from any information or suggestion in this book.

Favorite Desserts made VEGAN!;
100 Sweet Seductive Recipes
by
Lara Albrecht &
C.H. Barrington
Kathy Chrzaszcz

Published by:
Studio 5519,
1732 1st Ave #25519 New York,
NY 10128, USA

Contact:
info@studio5519.com

First Edition December 2018
(Version 1.0)
Updated December 4th, 2018

Illustrations:

Valentina Le

Photo Rights:

© Studio 5519

Dessert?

Selected!

Starter?

Oops...!

Main dish?

Phew...!

Inspirations wanted?

Take a look into the new book by the same authors:

Famous Dishes made VEGAN!

Vegans exist in all corners of the globe, united in their joy for delicious food, and that is what makes this book especially helpful. Cultures unite as we take some of the most delicious foods ever created from around the world – **and turn them vegan.**

Feast on dishes with treats that transcend continents and cross oceans. Think outside the breadbox and dig into a whole new world of flavor.

Made in the USA
Columbia, SC
16 December 2019